T0365716

A Mystic Looks at Life

Edgar N. Jackson
Lois E. Jackson, Ed.

Trafford rev. 02/25/2022

 www.trafford.com

North America & international
toll-free: 844-688-6899 (USA & Canada)
fax: 812 355 4082

To Estelle,
My partner on this journey of discovery

Table of Contents

Illustrations

PREFACE

by John Carr

You are about to read a remarkable book by a very amazing man. To be asked to write a few lines for Edgar N. Jackson's autobiography is an honor that I will never forget. My own life was touched by the Rev. Edgar N. Jackson in several important ways over the years.

Edgar's first book was *This Is My Faith: An Introduction to the Christian Life*. When I went away to our annual conference church camp, Quinipet, as a high school junior in 1948, Edgar was the dean as he was when I went back in 1949. His first book published was used as our instruction/discussion book, and it contained many gems. Edgar produced many such gems over the years as a minister, a teacher, and a strong advocate for several kinds of social justice issues. There is consistency and a concern for human values in so much of his writing, yet I was amazed at the marvelous story that unfolded about his life and his work as it is shared in *A Mystic Looks at Life*. There is much to absorb and contemplate in the various chapters, even for those not acquainted with Edgar and his many produced volumes. For those who knew him very well, there will be surprises and special moments to again be touched by the man and his spirit, his concern for all humanity, and his struggles against injustice and bigotry. Edgar shared parts of himself that readers of his books could never be aware of, good surprises and well-crafted lessons coming to challenge us to grow, to reach beyond, and to commit to something better.

Among the many facets that Edgar shares in these chapters, there is an important part of Edgar that remains hidden or at least understated.

He had a tremendous sense of humor. One of my experiences of this was when we were side-by-side in a procession at our annual conference ordination service. I whispered to Edgar that I realized that I had no money for the offering and asked if I could borrow some. With a smile, Edgar turned to me and said that he was only carrying a dollar but he would be glad to tear it in half for me.

One of my final contacts with Edgar in person occurred when I was in an ongoing training program with Dr. Lawrence LeShan. Arriving for a conference held at Princeton, I was pleased to discover that Edgar was a co-presenter with Larry for that weekend. In each of their writings, you can just feel the admiration and friendship they had for each other.

One of my big regrets was my failure to go up and visit Edgar in Corinth, Vermont, when he invited me to do so. I missed a wonderful opportunity. My visit to Vermont did come later, but it was to attend Edgar's memorial service. In his writings, Edgar encouraged us to do the right thing, the important thing, when we had the opportunity, but once again, I learned one of his lessons too late. In reading the pages of *A Mystic Looks at Life,* I realized that there was still time to learn more and grow again from Edgar N. Jackson. His writing on an amazing life will not only give you insight into his journey but also will likely help the reader discover or rediscover their own amazing life.

Thank you, Edgar.

FORWARD

by Ray Stephens

I first met The Reverend Doctor Edgar N. Jackson through his book Understanding Grief when I was in the seminary. I met the man, Edgar Jackson, at St John's University in Saint Cloud, Minnesota when he and I were on the faculty of the summer training institute "Dying and Death" in the early seventies. We became fast friends. Our friendship lasted until his death. His wisdom continues to influence the way I think, the way I relate to the world, and to fellow human beings, and to God.

He was one of the most intelligent men I have ever known. He was a kind, gentle prophet and mystic. From the first day of our friendship we knew we were kindred spirits. However, we argued as much as we agreed on theology, psychology, and later on holistic approaches to health care. This gave color and texture to our friendship. In this relationship he helped me to understand mysticism and to recognize how it was a vital part of my being. When I go to Vermont I always go to his grave and have a conversation with him. I leave with a sense of wellbeing similar to the many times we were together in a variety of settings.

I read this manuscript the first time immediately after it was completed. We met and talked about it, and he made a lot of revisions on it before he died. When I read it again, I understood parts of it that had been difficult for me years ago. Reading it warmed my heart and again filled my soul with affection and appreciation for this wonderful man. This book will serve the philosopher as well as the first-time reader of mystical truths. If one is seeking to understand the mystic's way of organizing the world, this book will help. If one is seeking to understand the mystical as it manifests in physical reality, this book will help.

Edgar Jackson lived with a constant awareness of his existential reality while being fully aware of the transcendent at the same time. I know very few people who have achieved this level of awareness. The 'clinical vignettes' of his interventions with a host of needy people are the richest parts of this book. They allow the reader to experience the man who was pastor, educator, healer, world traveler, and a friend. In his many roles he was always a friend. He allowed peership with the same gentleness that he sought peership with physicians, clergy, professors, and businessmen.

He was truly a 'people person.' He genuinely loved his fellow human beings. Wherever he was, he could have a conversation with a distinguished professor on one side and a farmer on the other, and never miss what these persons were sharing with him. I saw him listen to a farmer whose tractor would not start as intently as if he were listening to a person tell him about their life-threatening illness. In that same event, I saw him lay his hands on the tractor, tell the farmer to try again to start it, the tractor started up instantly Edgar turned and walked away with a wide smile as the farmer sat there amazed. Neither of them said a word about what had just happened.

He was a humble man, and at the same moment filled with pride because he knew that he made maximum use of his abundant resources in every situation. He truly believed that people who sought his help and care would benefit by what he could give. Though I never heard him say this, he could have said, 'I have never felt underutilized by anyone in any situation I have found myself.' Only a mystic could say that with honesty.

Dr. Jackson had the ability to make any situation into a potential healing experience. This is the way of the mystic. I have been with him many times when he 'laid hands' on a person without any claim, and wondrous things happened. I have seen and heard him tell people things that he knew about them even though he had just met them because of his remarkable psychic ability. He accepted their gratitude with grace, and pointed them toward a transcendent reality in a way that was compatible with each person's belief system rather than make a claim for his own beliefs.

I wish there were more narrative about the life of this man. He was one of the finest storytellers I have ever known. I wish he had told more of his 'stories' of simply being a human being. However, this would not have been comfortable for Edgar. He believed that one tells one's story, not to record history, but to give meaning to the moment in which the story is being told. The stories he tells in this book will enable the reader to experience a new meaning about mysticism. Dr. Jackson's primary purpose in life was to enable persons to experience meaning and purpose in the simple act of living. The reader gets a much more accurate picture of the value of this man's life if this truth is incorporated into the reading.

Anyone who has had the privilege of caring for the dying knows that there is nothing one can do that is more sacred than 'being with' a person in the process of dying, particularly at the moment of death. Edgar Jackson practiced this fine art of human caring to the final moment in his life. He was as gracious to those who came to his 'sick bed' as he was when he made pastoral, and therapeutic visits to the bedside of a person who was dying. He was a minister to his last breath. In ways that transcend human understanding, on the day of his death he made himself known to people all over the world so vividly that they felt compelled to call his home in Vermont to inquire about his health. His spirit continues to minister to those of us who knew and loved him. This too, is the way of the mystic.

INTRODUCTION:

Last evening we sat with friends talking of life and those events that mark its years. I was past seventy-seven and the rest of our party was younger. They tried to persuade me that it was time to write my autobiography. In order to draw them out I pretended to have no enthusiasm for the project. Their response was that if I had learned something of value through the years I had an obligation to share it with those who might now be going through the process. I did not find such reasoning convincing because of my own experience, for I had wanted to seek my own way and make my own errors. If there were any fortunate steps to be taken in life I wanted the ventures to be my own. That I had had an interesting life I would readily admit though I would not urge others to follow in my footsteps. I firmly believe each person must strike out on the course that seems wise and take the consequences. Most of the things that had been unusual were not planned but were the result of happenstance.

I soon learned that the important events of life were largely out of my hands and much of life was tinctured with tragedy. This was assumed rather than thought out. When I was not yet a year old my older brother was victim of what we would now identify as a virus and was not able to survive the encounter. Then in the 1918 flu epidemic my younger sister was quickly subject to the disease so virulent in the climate of war and its perniciousness. So in the early years I was bracketed in acute grief and saw and felt the power of that emotion though I had little understanding of its impact. I soon felt that life was not secure and that I must look beyond human agency to find hope and help in this life. As a child, I was intensely religious and yet I was only tentative in my feelings of security. The whole family was engaged in a constant struggle against a relentless fate. When I decided to try out for football my mother discouraged me and my father tried to remain neutral. Late at night I heard them discussing it. My mother in a voice filled with emotion asked, "Haven't we had enough without asking for it?" And my father said," We can't let our fears destroy his chance to live his own life". So the lines were drawn. Though I was never a good football player I enjoyed the game and understood its broader meaning. They were growing-up years in life and understanding.

A sense of self and one's sense of family are two sides of the same coin for their intermingling is inevitable and constant. I am well aware of myself and my own experience as uniquely mine, but I am also bound by that awareness of the fabric of family that intrudes powerfully and inevitably on every aspect of being. A relative who is profoundly influenced by genealogy is proud of the fact that he can trace a line of descent from Charlemagne. The fifty or so generations that intervene certainly give plenty of room for the good, bad and indifferent of individual and group history. Let us skip most of the events between these earlier times and our family participation in the happenings on these shores. It seemed our ancestors missed the boat and did not arrive in New England until 1630 and did not stay long. Some went to Southold on the north fork of Long Island and others kept going south until they settled in Virginia. The Long Island branch stayed pretty close to their New England ties but did mingle with the Dutch as they moved closer to New York. Jonathan Edwards and Aaron Burr were related to that part of the family. Those who went south cast their lot with others who ventured west and were active in the affairs of Kentucky, West Virginia, Ohio and Tennessee. Simon Kenton, Andrew Jackson, Stonewall Jackson and even defenders of the Alamo were all part of that restless family. Where the Dutch influence was great there were stolid citizens with a few mavericks like Walt Whitman. My mother shared the Dutch-English heritage as my father claimed some of the family traits of those who were predominantly English with a touch of the Scotch-Irish that made up the basic stock that crossed the Cumberland Gap and went west. That background led to the mixed involvement in social affairs by farmers, clergy and schoolmasters with an occasional sally into politics. Many of these early settlers chose land that was strategically placed and became the centers of towns and cities. The lawyers for the railroads saw to it that these lands became property of the eastern developers and the settlers were soon removed. They went further west or became satisfied with their lesser lot. Some of those who were the offspring of the first settlers who ventured west started a reverse movement toward the east and when they came to eastern universities were satisfied to stay in the more stable communities of the original colonies. So I was brought up in the environs of New York and as soon as it was possible moved to the hills of Vermont. This quickly became my home base as I traveled millions of miles about the country and the world lecturing in 35 countries and using modern modes of travel to find a country without boundaries.

My father was a minister and quite mystical in his nature. He met life and its vagaries with equanimity. He was unfailing in his support for the underdog. In the early 1920's when the Ku Klux Klan was exerting considerable influence he announced a sermon on the Klan as Unchristian, Undemocratic and Un-American and faced a church full of white robed antagonists. I was much moved by this courageous stand against such a mob but they were cowed by the integrity of one man. It was an important lesson to me.

I learned a trade as an electrician to earn money for college and then enrolled at Ohio Wesleyan. My work schedule was so heavy that my academic adviser suggested I leave school but I ignored his advice and was doing straight-A work before I was finished and was given an honorary doctorate by my college. While in college I made the acquaintance of Henry David Thoreau who combined several qualities I admired. He was stubborn, an idealist, a mystic, a nature lover and a humanitarian. He set his own goals and was not easily diverted, loved nature and was not afraid to be different. A junior in college I wrote my first book length study and I have not finished it in 56 years, and I doubt if I ever shall. It was my first in depth encounter with another person and because he had been dead over 70 years I could react as a free agent and I could be entirely free in the transaction. When I left college he went with me. Thoreau has grown with me over the last fifty years and we have been constant companions during my lonely walks in woods all over the world. He has been part of my discipline and part of my freedom. He marked the completion of one phase of my growing up.

College was also a time of choices. To avoid a commitment to the ministry I majored in natural science. Geology seemed of all the scientific disciplines the least subject to emotions, so I gave myself fully to the earth, its slow change and its dependability. The professor, who was also a state geologist for Ohio was a gruff but concerned person who won my loyalty. When one day in casual talk he questioned his decision to become a scientist, I was thrown into turmoil, for my geologist was not a dependable guide. I spent a long summer working in a lumberyard and rethinking my life's direction. When I returned for my senior year my life was changed and I had set my course for good or ill and it proved to have large doses of both.

So I launched my career in the church, rather reluctantly but as the best possible climate for being both a mystic and a scientist fifty years before the time when such a blending was generally acceptable. Little did I know what that course would entail. But I have held constant and in the pages that follow I shall try to chronicle the varied events that have made a life full of pleasant and tragic events that have marked the course. I have learned things along the way that would guaranty a different way of venturing if I were to do it again. Yet I have few regrets and make changes in emphasis rather than direction. So let us get on with it and see in retrospect what has happened, and why.

Chapter 1

MYSTICISM AS A WAY OF LIFE:

I have now approached my seventy-eighth birthday and as I look across the years that are past and think of the experiences most memorable, certain things stand out. They are the things where the boundaries of my rational existence are stretched beyond the breaking point. I tend to be a rational being, and pay tribute to the things that make sense. In college I started out majoring in geology and gave my loyalty to those things that were of the earth, earthy and had the feeling of bedrock.

My geology professor was my model in thinking and acting. I took all of the courses available to me in that department and marveled at the illumination that came with the writings of Charles Darwin. With close to a religious devotion I gave myself to truth as it was measured by scientific exactness. I found security in the rationalistic-scientific premise mode of thought and nothing else seemed to satisfy my soul. I asked my professor of geology to inscribe my copy of Darwin's Life and Letters with some appropriate remarks, and he wrote "Darwin's Life and Letters is one of my best loved books because it shows the mind of a man who was an ideal scientific worker and the heart of a man who was simple, kindly, and modest: a combination of qualities of mind and heart which have made him one of the glories of the English race." Professor Lewis Westgate wrote those words in 1932; long before the Darwin-Wallace correspondence with its implications was brought to light. But it gives a clue to where my mind and heart were at that time in my life. And this same geology professor started the process that raised questions about the limits of the rationalist-scientific process for knowing truth.

One evening when we had spent the day with the state geologist of Ohio mapping the oil-bearing shale rock in southern Ohio we were sitting around the little country inn drawing up our maps and relaxing with casual conversation. I posed a question to Dr. Westgate. I said, "If you had your life to live over again would you be a geologist?" He pondered it a minute and then said, "No, I'd be a minister." We discussed his answer quite a while and the substance of his thinking was that there are plenty of scientists in the world but that our need was not for scientific truth but for spiritual truth. He thought if he had another trip around he would try being a spiritual leader. I earned part of my living singing baritone in the church he attended and many Sundays when the sermon was not gripping I looked at Dr. Westgate sitting in his accustomed seat and I wondered what he was thinking and why.

Part of Dr. Westgate's life was centered on the material and disciplines of science, but he was quite willing to agree that there was a large world beyond science that he could not ignore. As he grew older he paid more attention to the mystical dimensions of his own being. I too tried to bring those two disparate aspects of the process of knowing into a compatible relationship. I went on with my education with a strange dedication to science and reason while there was a strong inclination to question the traditional concepts of religion. I was sure that there was a large world of truth and meaning beyond science and reason but I was not sure of the methods to be employed to arrive at that more rarefied field of knowledge. I tried to find that other approach to truth through the church and for several years I had not seen my geology professor.

Then one night I had a vivid dream of him and he was alive and very present. I talked of it at breakfast and was exclaiming that it was as though he were there in person when the doorbell rang. It was Dr. Westgate and his wife getting an early start on their drive back from New England to the mid-west. He said that he had wakened in the night and debated with himself whether or not they should go out of their way to look me up. Finally he decided to try to locate me and pay a visit. We had a fruitful half hour before they started on their way and it was the last time we were together before he died. It was as though he used this last meeting to reinforce the mystical experience of a special kind of knowing.

I thought often of the events that seemed to be beyond coincidence that made the scientific mode of thought appear to be inadequate to explain some of the events of life. Events of this type happened more often and it seemed that the more I accepted the possibility of such happenings the more often they occurred. Shortly after this strange happening I had a meeting in New Haven of the pastor's group to which I was quite loyal. I never missed a meeting. This day I started for the meeting and something held me back. It made no sense but every time I started to go this strong impulse held me back. It was irrational but overpowering. I struggled with the impulse until it was past time for the meeting and then I went to work in my upstairs study. Then when there were no noises from the family I became suspicious and went to investigate. I found them lying unconscious, Estelle on the couch and my son, James, on the floor. I quickly assessed the situation and decided that gas was the cause.

I opened the front door and took my wife out and sat her on the porch where she could breath fresh air, and took my son upstairs to a room that had windows opened and the door closed. I started giving him artificial respiration but he did not respond. After awhile I held him upside down and spanked him. He gave a couple of gasps and then started to cry. I took him crying in my arms downstairs and onto the porch where I could supervise both my wife and son and when I was sure that they were breathing regularly and well I called our family doctor who came immediately. She checked them out and verified my suspicions of gas poisoning. She said that she would have to do more tests to see if there was any permanent brain injury but for the present all she could guarantee was that they would have severe headaches for a while. We had a heating repairman on the job that day and they found the metal shield of the furnace was eaten through so that carbon monoxide gas was being piped into the living room. When it was all over I was left with the problem of explaining the strange behavior that kept me from going to the meeting, as I would have returned home to find my whole family asphyxiated. I was again aware of a way of knowing that was beyond the confines of ordinary rational-scientific ways of gaining knowledge. I was left with these experiences whose significance I could neither deny nor explain.

In a few years I was caught up in the strong emotional stresses of the war in Europe and Africa. Early one morning a physician in the medical corps burst through the hole in the wall that marked the boundary of the space allotted me as a Chaplain's office. He was obviously emotionally distressed as he blustered out the words "tell me all you know about immortality and tell me quick". I knew him well and this outburst was not like the calm, official medical presence he usually presented. So I slowed him down and said to tell me all about it starting at the beginning. He tried to do this but it was not easy to control his emotion. He said that he was reporting to operations where he was to accompany an ambulance plane that was to take a load of litter cases to a base hospital from our station in the Balkans. He said he was walking along with another officer when something happened to him that he never had happen before. He used medical terms to describe it. He said something broke in upon his consciousness just like a moving picture. It was a planeload of litter cases. They were caught in a weather front and were lost along the coast of Italy. Then without warning they flew right into a mountain. He said he could see it all as if he were a spectator. The tail section broke loose and went its own way down the mountain. Everyone on the plane was killed instantly and he said he just rubbed his hands together as if that task were finished and he walked away from the wreckage. He said he wanted to know what happened and where did he walk to? He then explained about his feelings. He said nothing in his life had ever seemed as real as this event. He came forth with a multitude of questions and I did not have any inclination to try to answer them as he asked them.

Our first task seemed to be to try to cope with his anxiety and so we tried to talk it out. When he had calmed down some, I asked him what the vision meant to him. He said that it was a preview of what was going to happen to him and his load of litter cases and he was sure of that. We explored how he was so sure. He said this was a special kind of assurance but he had no proof. I asked if he was so sure and as a medical officer in charge he had command authority to cancel the flight for the day. He thought awhile and then shook his head saying that he couldn't do that for they would think he was suffering from flight fatigue. So we talked for a couple of hours while they were preparing the plane and loading the litter cases. Our talk was earnest and dealt with many subjects, religious and parapsychological, for he was a serious thinker as well as a scientist and Jewish philosopher. We satisfied many of his questions but not those that had to do with his deep assurance of the validity of his vision.

I walked with him to the plane and again raised the question of canceling the flight. He shook his head a final negative as he pulled aboard. Soon they were rolling down the runway and were airborne. I stayed near operations most of the afternoon and checked the progress reports. Finally they reported a bad weather front and limited visibility. Finally

5

there was a loss of contact. Investigation showed that the accident occurred as the physician had previsioned it, with one exception. A sergeant who had been airsick went into the toilet at the tail of the plane and upon impact it broke off and although he was injured he survived. Apart from that it happened as the medical officer had foreseen it that morning and in his agitated state had reported it to me. Again I was aware of a kind of knowing that was baffling in its implications about the mind and spirit of man. But also I was deeply troubled because I had not seen more clearly the tragic nature of the ensuing events and had not been able to weaken his resolve to continue the flight. The knowledge was accurate but not forceful enough to make the corrective action adequate to prevent the tragedy.

Soon I was to have more of a burden on my conscience due to impotent psychic perception. We had moved our airbase to the south side of the city of Athens at Kalamaki. I was scheduled for a routine trip down to one of our out stations on the island of Crete. I had put my equipment aboard the plane but when I tried to get aboard a strong physical force held me from getting aboard. It was a powerful force such as I had not felt before. It was stronger than I was and although I made repeated efforts I could not break through the restraining force. I was puzzled by what was happening and decided to cancel my trip. I went around to the place where I could speak to the pilot and said I was scratching and would go with him on the next trip two days hence. I went back to my office to ponder these strange events and did not realize how the time had raced by. I happened to be the ranking officer on base that day and a messenger from operations raced up with the news that the plane had crashed in the Mediterranean and a request for orders. I said prepare another plane at once with plasma and other rescue materials for immediate departure with medical personnel. The doctor didn't want to go but I asked him to accompany me and he did. This time there was no force restraining me. We were soon at the spot where the plane had sunk and some fishing boats were on the spot and had tried to save some of the survivors. We landed at Hiraclion and went immediately to the local hospital and got to work as best we could with the injured. Four men went down with the plane.

It was late evening before we had time to think of the events of the day and their meaning. There were again unexplainable as well as tragic factors to consider and I was impressed with the partial knowledge that affected my behavior. Twice in two months I felt guilty for being in possession of information that was essential for the welfare of others but not realizing its meaning. The psychic information came in bits and pieces and I was not able to interpret its full meaning. The burden of that knowledge was hard to bear and I sought for years to find the meaning of the events and to strengthen the meanings that could have value for others. I was a rather untrusting person as far as psychics were concerned. I wanted to test out all of the possible scenarios rather than to leave the initiative with someone else. But I thought I could manipulate circumstances enough to get the benefit of psychics without giving away my own goals.

Some time had passed but I still had the same questions and they remained unresolved and undiminished in intensity. The war was over and I was back near New York when I read in the New York Times that Arthur Ford was speaking there and staying at a local hotel. I went to hear him speak remaining near the back of a large auditorium and doing nothing to give away my identity. I was impressed by the quality of his lecture. He was a clergyman and had a reputation for integrity. I left immediately following the lecture and spoke to no one. The next day I called the hotel and spoke to him, again giving no identification and made an appointment to meet him in his room two days hence. When I arrived I again avoided giving any identification saying that that would be more appropriate after the session. He asked if I had brought my tape recorder. When I gave a negative answer he expressed regret for he said he was unconscious during the session and the only way he knew what happened was by listening to the tape. After a brief explanation of how he worked and what to expect he breathed deeply for a few minutes and then began to speak with French inflection attributed to Fletcher, his control. He quickly identified a young man present, as my son, who had died as the result of an accident in 1936. He immediately said that he had saved me from annihilation in the Eastern Mediterranean. Then he gave the circumstances of his death in 1936 that we had seldom mentioned. For three quarters of an hour he continued to give evidential material of a private and precise nature. I was too moved by the experience to talk much with Ford and left soon after. Much of the material he had supplied could not conceivably come from any other human source. I was obliged to assume that it came from a source that possessed an active intelligence that was conversant with my sense of time and space and as well was aware of my thought and feeling structure. I was actively on guard against any possibility of fraud or error. I made arrangements with Arthur Ford for another session and I must report that everything about it was disappointing for there was no evidential material forthcoming and I had no other session with him.

I had to come to the conclusion that the trance medium was a fallible source, sometimes revealing highly significant material and at other times completely unsatisfactory. It then became a matter of careful evaluation of the fruits of that form of communication so that the wheat could be separated from the chaff. I eventually became better acquainted with Arthur Ford and spent hours discussing his ability as a medium with all my doubts showing. He seemed to be quite as baffled as I was about how the whole process could be conceived. He appeared satisfied to believe that he possessed a talent or special endowment of consciousness that interested other people and he was willing to be used for the satisfaction of their needs. He personally held some doubts of his skill and settled for the idea that as he was in a trance state when he functioned he was not responsible for either his success or his failure.

However I was not satisfied to leave the matter in that unsettled state. I wanted to know more and so I set about inquiries that have commanded the attention of my life and thought for the past third of my years. I have rethought the experience of my earlier years with an effort to organize it into coherent segments. I have tried to trace the mental and emotional sources of my behavior. I have spent much time and thought in trying to penetrate the meaning of my experience. My formal study and also my informal experience and explorations have sought to bring meaning to those events of my earlier years that charged me with guilt and also filled me with wonder. I wanted to know all that I could know about this portion of my life and its intriguing and baffling nature. If I were going to find the answers that satisfied my soul, I was sure I would have to ask the right questions. My scientific study and inclination would certainly be a help in bringing the questions into sharp focus. My mystical explorations would help to supply the intuitive insights without which I could not proceed far.

The first part of my life provided me with the raw material I needed for my further explorations. It was now my task to carry my study and examination of phenomena further and refine the meanings that were related to them. It seemed to me that one of the requisites to this exploration was freedom of mind and emotion. To this end it seemed that I must retire from the church and the traditional limitations of thought processes that were involved. I had received much from its life and teaching but I realized that as I moved into the future I must be on my own. This was done gradually without placing a burden on my family or friends. So the next few years were given to an effort to find some answers to the questions that had baffled me in my struggle to make my rational-scientific self feel at home with my intuitive-mystical self.

Chapter 2

GOD AND MY LIFE AS A MYSTIC

In writing my autobiography and trying to define the mystical relationships I have achieved, I feel that there should be a chapter on my idea of God, but the more I study the matter the less I seem to be certain of in some respects. But it is such an important area of thought that I should make some effort to give my thinking on the subject.

I had a childhood that was God centered. The God that filled my experience was real and present and exerted a major influence on every aspect of my thinking and acting. When my father prayed he was talking with what seemed to be a real person, who was closer than breathing and closer than hands or feet. Each morning as we gathered around the breakfast table my father would read a portion of the Bible and then we would all dismount and kneel at our respective chairs. My father or mother would take turns in offering a prayer and I well remember the time when I asked for my turn and from then on until I left home for college Tuesday morning was my time. As I recall it none of my siblings participated. I participated in a family ritual but I can remember that its meaning for me varied considerably through those formative years. I remember questioning the idea of God on logical grounds and I recall praying to my father's God for I didn't have one of my own.

In college we had a small fellowship of students who had an active religious life and we used to pray together, and as I recall the activity it was a sharing of commitment more than a designation of a role either by ourselves or some cosmic other. It was a time of easy compromise and my stance was fluid enough so that changes could take place with very little dislocation. As the atheist could make bold statements without assessing much meaning to them, so my affirmations on the subject would not carry much weight and might change quite often without involving my underlying belief in something that was acceptable to my family and peers.

I was committed to a positive emphasis in some sort of a cosmic projection and was willing to let it go at that. When it came to a career choice I thought more in terms of social service than real commitment. Actually I was more inclined toward a career as minister of music and was willing to put my musical skills and training to work in that way. But the full impact of the depression made itself felt in these years, and the musical idea didn't make sense when most church budgets cut down on music at the first financial pressure. So it was the easy thing to move toward the pastoral ministry in place of a musical emphasis. It does not seem to have been much of a problem but rather moving toward a goal in easy stages. In 1932, practical considerations had a primary claim on everyone's thinking and action. So while I continued my musical studies, by the end of the first year in seminary I was candidating for a church I could serve as I attended school. It did not seem to me then that God was a very important matter in the whole thing. The climate of the seminary assumed that student parishes were a necessary burden for small churches to bear and seminarians thought of student parishes as a meal ticket plus a good learning experience.

The first Sunday in my own parish gave me many impressions not the least of which was the congregation's evaluation of me. It was as if I were taking an oral examination. But the scrutiny worked both ways for I saw a young woman who was a church school teacher and a soloist in the choir and unusually beautiful and giving evidence of a singular personality.

I decided that I would have to give the matter my careful and serious attention. In a little over a year we were married and fifty-four years later I am still proud of my choice and the reasons for it. While I thanked God in a general way for my good fortune, I did not seem to think that a cosmic entity had much to do with the matter. A year later we were proud parents of a handsome and intelligent son. We were proud of what had been accomplished in so short a time. We were not ready do deal with tragedy and what happened a little more than a year later had profound theological impact. An accident took the life we so prized and brought the meaning of God into focus as nothing else in life had done. What did this death mean and how were we going to cope with it? Was it a purposeless act in a universe that was unconcerned? How could this apparently meaningless event be made the cornerstone of a theological system that was rational, that could make sense in a universe that was apparently without feeling or compassion?

I asked all of the questions that came flooding into my mind. It took me several years of asking all these questions and more to begin to find some answers that made sense. The new answers were quite different from the answers that I had found satisfying in the past. I came to the conclusion that the theological systems that had served human beings in the past were constructed to meet the needs of a universe viewed in small terms where a small concept of God fitted the rest of the small concepts. Our view of the universe was such that old ideas no longer served a useful purpose. The view that a cosmic personality with human characteristics had the capacity to be concerned about individuals on a third rate planet whirling about among the billions of solar systems no longer seemed to make sense to those who needed to think of a universe that made sense.

I finally came to the conclusion that such concepts could be relegated to those remnants of past thinking that were no longer relevant to the universe we had inherited and must come to terms with. I came to the conclusion that humans had constructed their theologies to meet the needs of their imaginations and needs. They need have no relation to reality as long as they meet certain needs of human seekers. It was then that I grew to be comfortable with the idea that theology was the projection designed to let people feel a meaning and purpose for the experience of living. Once they had posited that proposition they were free to build any structure that appealed to them. So I set about the task of trying to find a meaning and purpose for human existence which could take into account all of the incidents that occurred in the human experience, good or bad, wise or foolish. I was then able to choose the values and make my commitment to them and in effect create a life of my own that had the possibilities I sought without any chance of it being countermanded by any person or circumstance. I could choose the values I was in favor of and make my own value system that was secure in a world where so much was left to chance.

As I look back on this period of my life, I am aware that it is comparable to that period spoken of as the dark night of the soul. The world I had known and adjusted to had been shaken by death and I had to develop a new value system to survive in it. It was as if I had been living in two worlds, one of the adjustments that convenience had demanded of me, and the other which would not accept anything except what would be compatible with my new sense of the absolute of truth. I was obliged to jettison much of the furniture of my mind that had been uncritically accepted but no longer met my standard for truth. For a time I felt like a theological orphan but I gradually adjusted to my new psychology and cosmology and the personal dimensions of my world began to fall into place and the new world was a lot more comfortable than the old one had been.

Much of the suffering had come from the deep wounds of the spirit produced by acute grief. Recovery was slow and painful but the new view of life was more satisfying for me. It was as though I had to redefine each and every life situation and experience from a new perspective. I took pleasure in the fact that each new answer made more sense but I had the feeling that it was a lonely perspective, for my colleagues in the church were not willing to take the pilgrimage along with me. My conversations were usually friendly enough but they usually ended with some such rejoinder as this, 'but there are some things where you have to take it on faith' and I realized that that was the point of separation. It was not the point of recognizing the validity of faith but rather was the projection of mind that was worthy of the investment of faith.

I tried to develop a concept of faith that was not bound up with self-manipulation. I believed that there was a faith based on the wise commitment of life that would stand the test of intellectual examination. The first book I wrote was entitled "This is my Faith" and one of the last "The Role of Faith in the Process of Healing". They were efforts to define an intellectual projection in life that would increasingly prove the validity of a certain way of living. I felt that we could control our thinking and that if we did it responsibly life would show the benefits. This appealed to my mood of accepting responsibility for as much of the destiny of life as it was humanly possible. It also fitted my idea of the mystical for the individual could bring more and more of life into the realm of personal choice and cosmic possibility without destroying the integrity of the individual or the nature of ultimate reality. This way of looking at life and reality was assumed as a working premise and was operational at least experimentally. The more I lived with it as a tentative way of seeing things the more I was satisfied with it as a way of life that

I could accept critically and live with at the point of my inner integrity of being.

As far as my functioning within the church was concerned I had no difficulty for I set the parameters within which I would function and in preaching and pastoral work I was not obliged to compromise. But when the administration of the church asked me to compromise my integrity I found out that some elements of the institution were so intransigent that I had to make a choice between my internal being and the power of the institution. I tried every way I knew to bring the matter to an honorable compromise but found it was not possible and so withdrew from the fellowship and enslavement of the institution. I had seen too many who made the compromise and suffered from it and I chose the lonely way with integrity rather than keep up the collegial benefits with loss of relationship. My inner integrity involved my personal sense of God and it was something that was not up for compromise. My Idea of God was not determined by any group or compromise, for it was the ultimate for me. My theology was not an intellectual formula, an historical manufacture, a learned response, or a compromise of convenience. Rather it was the achievement of my total being, a definition of my essential self, and therefore it was not open to any limitation or compromise. This was where I learned the most about both God and myself. It was a lesson I spent most of my mature life learning. It was the most important learning experience of my life and made it possible to turn the dark night of my soul into the knowledge of a faith that stands any stress and a wisdom that meets all of life's needs.

It was at this point that I began to make a deeper and more careful exploration of mysticism. I wanted to make sure of the values that were basic to the commitment I was making. For it was going to be my ultimate commitment. It was going to be my ultimate structure of belief as both my scientific truth and my religious commitment. Science has a way of becoming a religion for some followers of the limited method employed by scientists. Often this comes about without a full awareness

15

of what is involved in the process. Science follows a precise set of rubrics as if it were committed to a religious conviction without realizing that there is something incompatible about that behavior. The scientist moves beyond his normal frame of reference when he considers things that are not bound by measurements of space and as science pushes out the boundaries of its explorations it begins to encounter a no-man's land where the traditional provinces of the two encountering forces become entwined.

The scientific study of religion runs into similar difficulties as it tries to put limitations on those things that are not easily reduced to measurements. It seems as if some language, such as the mystic uses, serves a valid purpose in bridging the gap between the purely measuremental and the direction in which it points. In his best thinking the scientist is always just a short step away from the metaphysical but that seems to be a step he cannot take without violating a major commitment. For instance in his book <u>Frames of Mind,</u> Howard Gardiner talks about a dilemma of the scientist in more mature years who seeks to find in metaphysics a brand of reality that is never found in pure science alone. The scientist resists the inclination of the maturing mind to move beyond a limiting frame of reference to find more space to expand the more reasoned accumulation of judgment and experience. Max Planck long ago observed that the scientist cannot help becoming a metaphysician when contemplating the question "why" for meaning always moves beyond the simple measurement that is the realm of pure science. When the "how" is compromised by the "why" a major change in direction is implied.

I was in the position of trying to find the middle ground where I could function with the discernment of a scientist on the one hand and the quality of spirit on the other. There seemed no way of doing it without practicing the discipline of the mystic, using all the capacity of the scientist with the added perception of the ability to see beyond to the meanings revealed. This led to an in-depth study of a subject in which I had long had an active interest. I was determined to know as much as possible about the human mind and its relationship to consciousness as a way of knowing and as the major discipline of the process of knowing so that the nature of mind could be brought to its finest realization. It was at this point that I thought I was able to come as close to a concept of God as it was possible for me in my quest for meaning. Here I was well beyond any revealed construct that could be put on from the outside where I was dependent upon the thinking of others. It was a way of perceiving ultimate reality, my ground of being as it were, where I would not violate either the dimensions of the physical universe as I knew it or the extension of my own consciousness as I was responsible for it and its devotion to truth both scientific and cosmic.

I was suspicious of traditional ideas of revelation yet mysticism and some of the insights that come with it share some of the phenomena of revelation. The mystic's perception brings together the energies of consciousness and the inventive-creative capacities of the mind in a way that makes something new—something that has not existed before. It is well within the range of the natural, the law and order of the universe at the same time that it brings unity and direction to mental activity. Mysticism is sometimes misunderstood as a nonrational process of the emotions. While the emotions are clearly involved, the mystical experience appears to be an integrative process in which mind, emotion, physiological endowment as well as cumulative perception are melded into a transcendent form of understanding supplemented by heightened awareness of relationships and meanings. While John Baille claims that revelation does not create something new but enriches what already exists, the mystical awareness shares the creative process and may well produce something that has not existed before. This would be true of the mystical experience of the artist, the musician, and the poet as well as the religious thinker.

I recalled my favorite professor of philosophy propounding a concept that I came to find helpful in my effort to create a theological concept that I found valid. There had been many ideas of God that I had outgrown and I had adjusted my life to this growing process. But I could not outgrow the concept of transcendence. The more I grew the more it grew and the more satisfying it became. It starts with a mental process and involves comprehension. The more the mind is able to comprehend the larger the mind's grasp of reality becomes. A child is at home in a small world because the experience of a child deals with this small world of experience. The growing experience of the child fits the world of growing experience. There comes a time when the growing does not keep up with the questions about life that seem pertinent. The minds of humans outgrew the universe that they had inherited and we had long periods of doubt and uncertainty. Individuals experience this uneven growth. My idea of God did not fit the universe my scientific framework of thought demanded. So I had to jettison the old framework and find another. I had to move beyond a personal concept of God that was a projection of a desire for human companionship in a cosmos constructed after my own heart's desire. The realization that there was something more important than my heart's own need and desire freed me to grow into the full possibility of transcendence. Each step of growth showed a greater possibility of achieving a perception that was not bound by what is known but rather invites a reach of the mind toward what is surmised. The nature of mysticism is found in that extension of the faculties of mind and spirit which willingly moves beyond the known to the unknown, the easily explained to the unexplained, the realm of the imagined to the world of the fulfilled as the ultimate meanings are achieved. The mystical awareness is carried to its ultimate realization in the mystical fulfillment.

We live in a day when every one of the senses is explored to see how it can be expanded. The telescope and the microscope give the eye a greater vision—the sensory refinement is able to see what has never been seen before. As Galileo's "tube" with its simple optical formula gave the stars a new closeness, so the electron microscope and the radio telescope bring to the mind's eye new perspectives of reality. As the cells of the eye are similar to those of the brain, so the function of the brain through the minds eye may add a new dimension for understanding the mysteries of science. The dividing line between the physical resource and its creative function may become increasingly tenuous and may fade away in a new amalgam of mind and matter. What Pierre Tielhard called the "omega point", the place where science and the questing spirit meet, may be achieved where the mystic spirit of science and religion become one. The apostles of this mystic achievement have gone before them. A whole group of courageous souls including Giordano Bruno, Blaise Pascal, M. Bergson, Henry Margenau and Pierre Teilhard have shown that the scientist and the mystic can be familiar with the same perceptions of reality without violating the boundaries of their disciplines. They can see the goal toward which both science and religion move. They can anticipate the amalgamation of disciplines that are compatible even before they are melded and can foresee the horizon that their mental projections anticipate. Instrumentalism and transcendentalism may appear to be in conflict as to their origins but not in terms of their ultimate goals.

Theology is always ultimately personal and private as one's own way of achieving ultimate meaning for the experience of living. No one can have any one else's theology. You may study a theology and try to make it your own but there is always that element of the individual that becomes a part of the amalgam. There are as many theologies as there are people. All of the strenuous efforts to produce correspondence are mere approximations for there is always the personal element that makes every approach to God and ultimate reality unique. A person's theology is the ultimate achievement of selfhood. I spent years discovering that basic truth. Not only did I find that my idea of God was intensely personal, but I also found that it was my right and privilege to achieve the idea that best suited my own integrity of being. In the long pilgrimage to my own idea of God I have finally found my way through to what is satisfying to my deep inner being. I may not be able to interpret it satisfactorily but I do not have to. This is my private domain. It was achieved at a great price. Nothing can now modify or diminish this hard won position in my inner life.

I think that there has been a large amount of human suffering endured at this one point, for much social turmoil and many wars have been fought over this point that cannot be established in any external conflict. Each person must make the God that will be paramount in life. The realization of that fact would at once lift a heavy burden from human kind. There may be joint efforts at worship but there must be primary responsibility for what goes on in the core of being where the consciousness reigns supreme. No person or organization can presume to determine or control this sacred point where deep speaks unto deep and where God is known in the consciousness of each individual.

As I outgrew the boundaries of a concept of God in the external and a concept of a being of the external universe, so I achieved a wholeness of spirit that became for me the ultimate reality. I had found my God and my peace deep within myself and it radiated out into all the universe through my awareness of the law and order that was everywhere revealed. That was sufficient to all my needs.

Chapter 3

MYSTICISM AND THE STRUGGLE FOR RATIONAL KNOWING

Mysticism is not so much a type of philosophical orientation as it is an attitude, a way of feeling and thinking about life in its totality. Science tends to be reductionist in its attitude for it uses only those forms of measurement that it can manipulate or restrict. But there is always more to life than can be measured by such restricted standards of measurements. Mysticism tends to be more inclusive in its perceptions as per Einstein's book <u>Cosmic Religion And Science</u> in which he makes intuition a major ingredient in scientific creativity. How the mystical consciousness comes about is not clear. Individuals tend to develop a mystical awareness as a result of the circumstances of life rather than a design. Charles Darwin was planning to go into the church that certainly involves some awareness of things mystical. But saturating himself in scientific measurements constantly caused some of the other habits of mind to be put aside. He remarked in his journal there was time when he enjoyed music and poetry but that his preoccupation with scientific things seemed to cause this aesthetic interest to wither away. Purely due to a switch in the circumstances of his life his interests changed and the voyage on the Beagle moves him and his interests in quite another direction.

Evelyn Underhill in her childhood was much interested in her inner being and its experiences and day dreamed. As she grew older this interest in inner and mystical experiences was pursued until it became the compelling concern of her life. She wrote many books elaborating this interest.

Eileen Garrett as a child In Ireland had a rich inner life and talked with the little people who were active in her imagination. She encouraged the growth of her inner being consciously or unconsciously and all the rest of her life she shared that interest. Any mystical inclination was encouraged and it seemed to develop actively under this toleration.

Although children differ widely in personality traits it is also quite obvious that circumstances in early life make a difference in how given traits are allowed to develop. As language use develops rapidly during early years so other forms of communication seem to be able to grow with encouragement under encouraging conditions. So the musical talent of a Mozart can make phenomenal strides in early years beyond all reasonable expectation. Other children may develop skill in communication in what is considered to be paranormal directions although the children involved are aware of nothing that is not within the bounds of the normal as they experience it. So the development of mystical abilities may be explained within the bounds of the normal. Life may provide the incentives for the fuller development of the skills of the mystical nature within the framework of quite usual experiences.

Experiments have been conducted to measure the presence of paranormal awareness in young children as they begin their years of normal training. Gertrude Schmeidler presided over tests that were applied to children in preschool sessions as well as first and second graders. What she found in checking several thousand of these children was that in preschool they seemed to have large amounts of paranormal awareness, and in the first grade they had begun to lose that capacity and by the time they were in the second grade there was very little of it left. The measure of conformative behavior that was required in the school system made it difficult for the gentle and unassertive qualities of the mental life to remain. Those who have mystical endowment such as Underhill and Garrett and comparable endowments such as Mozart seem to have gotten a good start in life and did not have an influence such as Darwin to change the course of their psychic growth.

But it is not always the scientific pursuit that has deadening influence on psychic development. We are now developing a crop of scientists who value the less materialistic mood of those who seek answers that cannot be driven into small corners. Henry Margenau is a case in point. He is considered by many to be the top philosopher of science in the world today, and yet he is deeply concerned about nonmaterial concerns of those who search the frontiers of knowledge. I sat across the table from him at a conference in Majorca and watched how his mind worked in response to questions raised during a week of sharing the basic considerations of a group of top scientific thinkers. Again and again the boundaries of scientific considerations were quickly reached and the scientists moved on to metaphysical considerations.

How do we know the truth? How does the mind work? What are the boundaries within which we can surely work in considering nonphysical reality? Such questions lead more quickly to the mood of the mystic than to the traditional scientist. We have a blending of disciplines so that old landmarks are valid no longer and new boundaries for the searches of the human mind must be established. The moods of this present day search are defined by a title of a book by Henry Margenau written in collaboration with a psychologist Lawrence LeShan, VANGOGH'S SKY AND EINSTEIN'S SPACE. The approach of the crude materialist is quickly outdistanced by the contemplation of such alternatives. The materialist cannot function as well with these vistas as the mystic.

Michael Polanyi starts the mind thinking in quite different directions when he talks of the Tacit Dimension. We create a world that is different for us at least by the very act of creative thinking. In tacit knowing there are given a series of illustrations of the way we know things but cannot say how we know. The administering of electric signals on the repeating of certain syllables can be used as an example. The syllable is known by the total organism but there is no way of identifying it before the spontaneous reaction occurs. The same thing is shown in facial recognition for we may be able to recognize thousands of faces but would have trouble describing accurately more than a dozen or so. Some unknown way of knowing seems to be operating to sort out faces and the ability to know. Often this problem of knowing shows up in court proceeding when a witness is asked to make an identification and is assured in mind that the capability is there but when faced with the actual person confusion arises as the many faces are not able to separated from the one. Psychologists identify the type of recognition as subception. This form of knowing has some of the characteristics of habitual acts for the total being is able to act with tacit knowing.

I once counseled a concert pianist who had lost the capacity to memorize music. He was at one time able to perform an extensive repertoire when something snapped and he could not play at all. It took a long rest and a slow rebuilding to approximate former skills. Any skill involves a considerable amount of tacit knowing or subception. The type of knowing that the mystic employs is not foreign to this type of tacit perception. This can unite with our preconscious experience in enriching our experience of knowing at the point of mystical knowing. There may be very few meaningless experiences but their meaning may be lost among those myriad sensations that go to make up the tacit knowledge. Sometimes these sensations are so subtle that they are not consciously perceived. With refined instrumentation these minor muscular actions

24

are recorded and are comparable to subliminal sensations that are accumulated but not consciously recorded. It becomes obvious that all our knowing is achieved through the complicated equipment of our bodies and its nervous system. This comes to a focal point in the ten thousand million cells of the brain that through their many interactions produce further interactions that cannot be calculated. But every second these interactions take place beyond the realm of consciousness. These actions of consciousness are but a tiny fraction of mental activity. The body may not know precisely the nature of the complicated process being carried on within it but there is a sum total awareness that is expressed in a form of tacit awareness that is observed in the nature of mystical awareness.

It is perhaps most clearly seen in what we call moral consciousness. Kant was so impressed by this moral consciousness that he attributed to it a cosmic source. We accumulate so much moral awareness in the racial consciousness that it clearly takes on a quality that cannot be attributed to any individual awareness. Not only can we know more than we can tell but we act on the basis of knowledge that we cannot explain and seem to be entirely comfortable about it. One cannot learn to play baseball by reading a rulebook alone for the skill in the game is dependent on the knowing that cannot be explained. Plato considered tacit knowledge as the experience and knowledge acquired in previous lives, a concept that is not generally accepted today. Many times in history there has been a conflict between tacit knowing and "revealed" truth and there is still vigorous contention between fundamentalist religionists and the frontiers of scientific thought. Also a body of tacit knowing can be obliterated by a major traumatic event. A person may have driven a car for years before an accident had destroyed confidence in driving so that never again was it possible to take the controls. Much in life may be in this borderland between the known and tacit knowing where we are not able to affirm the truth but act as if we were sure of the truth of our knowing. The mystic very often cannot prove scientifically the source of knowledge but acts on the basis of tacit knowledge that has its own assurance. Often the motives for scientific research are found in the tacit knowledge that is assumed as the basis for the more explicit knowledge that is sought as the end result of research. But any research must begin with an impulse to know that it is fed by a form of tacit knowing that inspires the research and can keep it going. And when the research comes to a dead end, as is often the case, it does not mean that the tacit knowing is at fault but rather that the plan of action was inadequate and that the problem needs a new perspective. The kernel of truth lurking in the formulation of the problem may have been ill conceived but the effort of the consciousness to give expression to it may need many experimental expressions before it finds the one that attests to its validity.

Some relationships between mystical awareness and the stimulus of great stress seem to be related to the behavior that is its byproduct. Yet we tend to avoid stress where possible and so may miss many of the mystical experiences that we might otherwise have. We avoid the experiences that might produce the creativity of the mystical.

Hans Selye who has researched matters of stress and health in depth says quite clearly that stress is not something to be avoided for the complete freedom from stress is death itself. "From the point of view of its stress-producing or stressor activity, it is immaterial whether the agent or situation we face is pleasant or unpleasant. All that counts is the intensity of the demand for readjustment or adaptation."

Several years ago I wrote a book, Coping With the Crises in Your Life, which was an effort to evaluate both the creative and destructive responses to the stress points of life as they were experienced at differing stages of life. In a review of this book a cancer research specialist, Dr. Lawrence LeShan, observes: "Two of the best kept secrets of the twentieth century are that everyone suffers and that suffering can be used for growth and 'becoming'." We have learned much about wiser ways of living life and skills for coping with destructive stress. But we have much to learn about the positive use of stress for improving our skills as creative human beings.

If "stress is the nonspecific response of the body to any demand made upon it" we begin to understand much of the behavior that might at first seem puzzling. Yesterday I spoke with a man who had come in second in a marathon. The thing that seemed to gratify him most was that his wife and the mother of his three children had come in first among the women contenders. Anyone who has won or even run the course in such a grueling test of endurance knows something of the self-inflicted pain that is a part of it. Yet there is much more to the race than the pain that is endured for there is the knowledge and satisfaction of mastering the coping skills that confront the stress and achieve mastery over it.

Hunters enduring cold feet and aching muscles in the wilderness, adventurers taking long and lonely treks or sea voyages, and more gentle sports enthusiasts share a common sense of self-mastery as they contend against themselves in the struggle for personal adequacy in life. The absence of this form of stress creating activity is without doubt one of the major restraints on creativity.

In my role as a spiritual guide I see quite often the problem of the divided consciousness, one part quite rational and coherent and the other holding to perceptions of reality that are quite at variance with rational perceptions and logical conclusions. This divided consciousness is supported by the history and tradition of the church as an organization and by its desperate effort to hold on to its role as verifier of both the rational and irrational at the same time. This has led to some disquieting claims in the past, none more at variance with rational process than the claims of the church in support of the virgin birth. Here the claims of tradition have been rejected, the New Testament evidence denied, to support a claim of the Church that has no verification and seems to need none except the claim of the Pope to be infallible when speaking ex-cathedra.

27

The problem of most of those coming into a pastoral encounter centers upon questions of meaning or meaninglessness. They may be introduced or camouflaged by surface questions having to do with mood or manners, but they quickly lead to more substantive concerns such as why or why not. They move toward theology aesthetics or ways of knowing truth with certainty though the process may be tinged with diffidence or doubt. A colleague comes with a query about his employment. He is committed to a profession that seeks to save life rather than destroy it; yet he finds that the research he does is used to stimulate hostility and a warlike mood. His livelihood is threatened if he questions the motives of those who supervise his research. His professional future is in jeopardy if he aborts his research halfway to its conclusion. Innocent people who cannot know his thinking will suffer by his action. He is confused by several questions that he did not anticipate and could not reasonably be expected to foresee. He expresses the turbulence within by questions like "What now?" or "Why this?" One does not look at "what now?" long without realizing that value judgments come in many varieties— some explore theory- some are practical and others are self-centered.

We live in a day when every one of the senses is explored to see how it can be extended. The telescope and the microscope give the eye its greater vision—the sensory refinement is able to see what has never been seen before. As Galileo's "tube" with its simple optical formula gave the stars a new closeness, so the electron microscope and the radio telescope bring to the mind's life new perceptions of reality. As the cells of the eye are similar to those of the brain, so the function of the brain through the mind's eye may add a new capacity for understanding the mysteries of science. The dividing line between the physical resource and its creative function may become increasingly tenuous and may fade away in a new amalgam of mind and matter.

Mysticism and the insights that come with mysticism tend to share some of the phenomena of revelation. The mystics perception brings together the energies of consciousness and the inventive-creative capaci-

28

ties of the mind in a way that makes something new-something that has not existed before. It is well within the range of the nature, the law and order of the universe at the same time that it brings unity and direction to mental activity. While John Baillie claims that revelation does not create something new but enriches and enhances what already exists, the mystical awareness shares the creative process and may well produce something that has not existed before. This would be true of the mystical expression of the artist, the musician and the poet.

Mysticism is sometimes misunderstood as a nonrational process of the emotions. While the emotions are clearly involved, the mystical experience appears to be an integrative process in which mind, emotion, physiological endowment as well as cumulative perception are melded into a transcendent form of understanding supplemented by heightened awareness of relationships and meanings.

Sir John Eccles sought to discover the process by which the physical phenomena became nonphysical. Perhaps this is best illustrated by the auditory sense. A physical stimulus, the waves in air, is projected to the area of refined skin known as the eardrum. Then it is projected through a fluid and a set of perfectly balanced minute bones to an area of nerve tissue, the auditory nerve. From that point on an electrochemical process takes over and the transmission from the part of the auditory nerve attached to the outer ear goes through a transformation. The electrochemical becomes a participant in the inventive-creative as the nature of the impulse changes on its way to the auditory cortex. The basic question Sir John poses is, by what means does the activity of the brain, the physical entity, become transformed into mind that appears to be the nonphysical process, which moves into the mystical realm of organization of consciousness. It also makes relevant another question basic to the understanding of the mystical phenomenon, could not the process be reversed so that the non-physical can condition and modify the physical and material aspects of being? Some have said that the body is the mind in action physically. If we can assume a two-way movement of the electrochemical and inventive-creative process in reverse it would answer many of the long standing problems related to the nature and function of consciousness.

When one approaches the question of survival of bodily death, there are three ways of considering. First is the anthropological where the experience of the race has been formulated in human consciousness and found expression in persistent modes. Second is the psychological where humans have tried to formulate an idea of survival in terms of human experience. And third, is the result of brain studies such as those of Lord Adrian and Sir John Eccles, where the inadequacy of reductionist approaches very quickly manifest themselves.

One can disregard the results of anthropological study at their own hazard. For thousands of years men have approached their surmise about the soul with projections in time and space. While this has no significance as far as measurement is concerned it does have meaning as far as the significance of the very concept is concerned. Wherever there has been an effort to see life in terms of its meaning there has been a formulation where certain concepts tend to reappear. Even in places where there has been no correspondence and no relationship certain concepts reappear constantly. If we are to disregard these correspondences we do it at the expense of an awareness of how important the racial wisdom may be. We can easily discount the results of primitive thinking but we cannot ignore the racial wisdom that may be behind the thinking. Primitive man had insights that were valid though his formulation of them could not escape his perception of cause and effect. When he gets beyond this primitive formulation he may have a clearer understanding of the forces that motivate his thinking. The process by which he arrives at basic understanding draws on wisdom that is not dependent on cognitive processes as much as it is dependent on precognitive awareness.

In the psychological process it is important to see how the mind thinks of itself in trying to perceive its function. One cannot ignore the processes by which one seeks self-understanding. Even if the product of that self-understanding is inadequate. Invariably efforts to gain insight through a reductionist approach limit perception rather than expand it. And limited perceptions invariably defeat their own process. The process of reducing automatically shuts off areas of insight and understanding. Whether the results of reductionism are valid or not the method leaves something to be desired.

Recent brain studies show incontrovertibly that in the effort of man to function in terms of his knowledge and use of his brain, the result always falls short of his possibility. It may be that the thinking of the Aboriginal is just as valid as the thinking of the supposedly sophisticated user of the brain. So it may be that the mystical awareness of Sir John Eccles or Lord Adrian comes closer to reality than the reductionist thinking of their detractors who make light of the cognitive process while assuming that their own limited wisdom is a valid explanation. They do not recognize, however, that their own limited cognitive process limits their wisdom.

Chapter 4

MYSTICAL DIMENSION OF EDUCATION

My father was my first formal teacher. Long before I was considered old enough to attend school my father set aside a portion of each day for me to study and learn. I looked forward to this time of day for it was a time of adventure and sharing with one who was important in my life. He seemed always to have a feeling of partnership in whatever we did and he had a way of encouraging my development so that I felt a part of whatever our learning skills revealed. Learning to read was an achievement that was filled with magic as a few black marks on a page could tell me something. When I was old enough to go to school I was moved right into the second grade for I was already reading beyond my years. My father and I had made an adventure out of arithmetic for he never gave me an answer to a problem but made the finding of the answer a game of wits which invited words of commendation for the right answer but also for the proper method. I was eager for the exploration of the growing edge of my awareness and found that the routine of learning was rather depressing when 1 had to slow my educational process to the level of my peers. Years later, the testing to which I was subjected revealed that my capacity was quite a bit ahead of the accepted level of my schoolmates.

While I did not put too much stock in IQ findings it was reasonable to make some measurements that showed capacity and the agility of the mind. The advantage of a good start and proper motivation was clearly shown in my case and the fact that my father had spent time in what was then called a normal school was to my advantage. Because we lived in New York State we were all subject to state exams by the board of regents. Because I was able to get a mark of 100 on my first regents' exam, I was given the rest of the exams and because I was able to score 96 average, I was graduated from grade school at 12 years of age even though I was the smallest in the class. This was no advantage when I wanted to make the football team made up of husky Polish and Italian boys who had no trouble tipping the scales to 200 pounds. The best I was ever able to do was become substitute end at 120 lbs. on a line that averaged well over 200 lbs. and all I had going for me was speed and endurance. But I had spent eventful years in public schools and won prizes in English and History although not much else of distinction in a large city high school where I was graduated at 16. Because I was so young I decided to go to work and learn a trade and make money toward my college education. I choose to learn a trade as an electrician and I took to it readily. After four months I was assigned a helper and was put in charge of wiring new houses. The boss came around once or twice a day to check things out and gave me a feeling of being a worthy workman by seldom making a suggestion and often giving me words of approval. The skills I developed then have stood me in good stead and I have used my electrical knowledge in many ways all of my life.

At 18 I was ready for college. I had grown a lot and developed skills and coordination that were important for my self-assurance. I entered a midwestern town on a rainy September morning where I knew not a soul except myself. Then I had the time of self-testing that was met with interest and skill that were surprising to myself. Not only was I well started in my education but also I found satisfaction in my work. I found several jobs that supplemented my income and made it possible to withstand the economic collapse that came along in November of my first year in college. It was not the best time to earn my way through college. My faculty advisor recommended that I drop out of college until economic conditions became improved. The first of many times I refused to take the advice given me. It was a struggle and I soon learned what it was like to experience hunger but I also learned that there was little that I could not endure with determination and belief in myself. By the end of the first year I was a youth worker in one church, a member of a quartet singing in another church, desk clerk in the library, operator of a dishwasher in the girls dormitory, janitor for nights in the school of music with a number of odd jobs that filled in my time summer and winter. When school let out I had jobs driving a lumber truck or working with construction crews except one summer when I worked as a stevedore. I learned what physical exhaustion could mean. The economic struggle was constant, but it was an education in and of itself. By the time I finished college I had worked at a dozen different types of gainful labor. It was an important part of my training for life.

Yet the important part of my college experience was the people I had encountered. There were a dozen or so persons who made a difference that lasted throughout my life. My father had studied at OWU a generation before me and had taken the first course in philosophy taught by Trumball G. Duvall. I took the last course that he taught some thirty years later. His rich perspective of life and his wisdom as he interpreted it were treasured memories and his concept of transcendence was a cornerstone of my philosophical system. It was the point at which I continued my intellectual growth when the logical framework reached it's outside boundary. This was basic to my view of mysticism and I have been thankful for a system that granted me a vision beyond the

framework of materialism. When Duvall retired, a young man just out of
Columbia took over with an instrumentalist point of view. His theme of
creative intelligence brought me in contact with the mood in philosophy
that was then prevalent and I quickly made its mood mine. Lawrence
Sears was a good teacher and he encouraged my personal growth. He
taught by the skill with which he asked questions that kept pushing
out the frontiers of knowledge. At the same time that he was using the
Socratic method of teaching in philosophy my geology professor, Lewis
Westgate, was using a similar method in science. Between the two I was
getting a good basis in dialectic thinking. Another philosophy professor
introduced me to quite a different way of thinking and when I took his
course in aesthetics I found yet another dimension of mystical thinking.
I found that the artist had a valid way of thinking of life and its meaning
which was more direct than the dependence upon verbal symbols and
could be employed as independent of verbal symbols or to supplement
types of symbolization.

An unusual conference took place the first week of my senior year at
college. My advisor told me that he had talked with my other professors
and they had concluded that it would serve no useful purpose to have
me attend regular classes for the year but would make more sense to do
independent study with a session with my advisor every week or two to
see how things were going. He said "One of your papers last year was
the finest paper I have ever known to be turned in by an undergraduate
student, and I have the feeling that anything we would suggest would
only tend to impede your independent study. " So it was agreed that I
would be on my own for the final year and that I would use the faculty
as I saw fit for the ensuing year. I was free to call for help if ever or as
often as I might want, but I accepted the challenge offered with enthusiasm. I immediately prepared an outline for the year's study and had it
approved. And then I started a far ranging use of the faculty to explore
in personal interviews any areas of my study that I felt had been slight-
ed. It was a glorious year with nothing lacking but my own stamina. A

bout with the flu caused me to abandon my ice cold sleeping room for the warmth and tender care of Prof. Duvall where I was nursed back to health in a couple of weeks.

Part of my education was an ever-present interest in music. I had studied piano for four years, the organ for three years and before I was finished with formal musical study seven years of voice. My recovery from the flu was interfering with my preparation for a senior recital I was planning to give later in the spring. I was going to mark my development in an art form that had a special appeal to me. I was going to sing in four languages as well as ancient English and its modern equivalent. An extra effort made it possible to finish all assignments on schedule. This study in applied art was a reasonable supplement to my studies in aesthetics.

My best scholarship offer was from a theological seminary in Madison, New Jersey. I attended for two years that took quite a bit of stamina for it was like returning to high school after the college experience. The return to keeping notebooks after years of independent study was supposedly to bring various types of college preparation into a common standard for the seminary. I tried to make the best of their academic wasteland but it was a constant struggle. Two years of good voice training was beneficial and I set myself the task of reading the twenty volumes of St. Thomas' Summa Theologica. I skipped many sections that did not seem relevant but it was a valid experience for understanding the Catholic experience. I found some scholarly souls who gloried in the atmosphere but I refused to take a required course in social theory that everyone admitted was worthless, which ended in a conference with the academic dean who invited me to continue my studies elsewhere. I have been invited back to lecture quite often and my assessment of the school is that it has improved quite a bit with the years.

I then continued my travels to Union seminary, which was quite a different place with Reinhold Neibuhr, Eugene Lyman, Harry Emerson Fosdick and such luminaries. Here the mood was modern with current political trends taking major consideration. I valued Fosdick and kept up my friendship and it grew closer when he retired and moved to the parish next to mine where his visits were a rich personal experience. Eugene Lyman gave me a chance to make a major study of Cardinal Newman who was a distant cousin of mine and I wrote a paper on his mysticism that gave me a chance to compare his thinking with that of Thoreau and Emerson. I dipped my toe in the political mood of Union by studying with Harry Ward and Neibuhr who were stimulating but I found that I was really not that much interested in political matters as they were encountered in the parish. There was so much room for superficial thinking and emotion without careful thinking. I considered my year at Union to have been well invested but it was still not quite what I was looking for so I transferred to Yale where there was a climate of scholarly interest blended with a genuine interest in a ministry of helping people find a healthful philosophy of life.

At Yale I was able to find a blending of disciplines that was to use all of my energies for three years and fill me with a desire for even more disciplined studies in human personality and its development. By using the full possibilities of the shared relationship with the graduate school I was able to take courses in other departments that supplemented my work in the divinity school. The professors might not have had such national and international renown as those at Union but they were more diligent as teachers in their concern with their students. I had matured and took my whole approach to school and my ministry with more perspective. I realized that each school has its own personality and there is a sense of achievement when the person or the student blends with the personality of the institution skillfully. I majored in two fields at Yale that invited continued study. They were communication and human personality. I had the advantage of taking work in what was then called the School of Human Relations, which was the current designation of the school of psychiatry. Here I was made aware of the fact that I knew very little about human beings and what made them tick. I had had considerable psychology but it was a generalized approach to human beings and was of limited use in assessing the characteristics of individual human beings. If I were going to be of use to human beings as I encountered them I would have to develop a skill in recognizing those human characteristics that would be aware of their needs as individuals and could observe those particular needs. So I spent my three years preparing myself for what I really wanted to do, and that was to go as far as I could go in developing the kind of understanding of people that would make it possible for me to minister skillfully to those people who came to me for advanced understanding. This was going to call for a specialized kind of understanding that I could not get at that time through seminary training. It involved the scientific understanding and approach to human beings. It would involve a completely different standard of judgment from that which was basic to seminary curricula. But I had to do it for this was the only way to integrate and achieve integrity to the study of personality.

So after spending three years in the very profitable environs of Yale I set out to find what was then not to be found in the theological seminary. I had the feeling that I was turning my back on the tradition that had nurtured me, but I felt I was mature enough to seek what I wanted without compromising my integrity or the concept of a ministry to people without any compromise. So I set off for the Postgraduate Center for Psychotherapy in New York, which has since changed its name. It was an eclectic school with a prominent faculty made up of members of faculties of other schools in the city and its environs. I was the only clergyman in a student body of about two hundred and fifty persons most of whom had graduate degrees in medicine, psychology or some related study of personality science. I had to answer a steady barrage of questions by other members of the student body, not unfriendly but generally amazed because they thought religiously inclined persons depended largely upon revelation rather than the methods of science. I found myself having to defend my belief in the value of religion but usually the mood was friendly and those who questioned me did it with a winsome attitude as if they would like to find a way to combine their scientific view of human personality with some religious assumptions about life. We spent long hours sharing our views and seldom became rancorous. They asked questions that were never asked in my former studies and they were basic to my philosophy of life. Some of their questions were beyond my easy answering and I had to do much rethinking of my premises and assumptions.

I began to find justification for their kind of thinking. I was obliged to raise questions about my assumptions and many times I was led to face the inadequacy of those I had followed for most of my life. I not only found that many of my assumptions did not stand up to careful scrutiny but also that many of them were antagonistic to the values of my deep religious convictions and had surrounded themselves with practices that could not be justified by any stretch of imagination. I must thank some of my fellow students at the postgraduate center for their insights and their willingness to take me on and challenge my bases for judgment and ways of thinking. I became convinced that I had been brought up in a way of thinking that was unexamined and that needed to be challenged. One would have thought that I would have examined my basic thinking in four years of college and six years of graduate study, but that was not the case in schools that were committed to acceptance of the sacred framework of some unchallenged and sacred premises. It was assumed that it was better to stop thinking than to think some thoughts that were unacceptable. There were many that figured out a way of getting their thought structure to conform to traditional ways of thinking and they were usually rewarded by being made professors. I now saw how the system had worked and I wanted no more of it for it was deceitful and could not stand the scrutiny of those who were determined to ask the unaskable questions. During my years of pastoral work I grew increasingly restless as I perceived that the theological base from which I had been taught to operate was at sharp variance from the goals I set for pastoral intervention. I was seeking to encourage growth toward maturity and independence and yet was expected to promote a theological stance that taught dependence and fostered immaturity. I wanted to encourage people to think for themselves and develop their own inner genius and yet it was assumed that one could find salvation only by adhering to certain orthodox and traditional patterns of thought. I wanted to help people discover an inner authority that could sustain life and achieve a philosophy of life adequate for all of life's circumstances, but I was expected to encourage a response to external authority provided by a defensive and self-serving institution. I sought to help people develop a loyalty to truth as a sound basis for living, but found that I was expected to teach and encourage a framework of falsehood that was built into the system.

I was seeking to teach inner peace and reconciliation as a way of life but found that on every side the institution that demanded loyalty fostered active conflict with other people and their ideas and projected an intransigence that manifested itself in an adversarial attitude against those who took another stance whether valid or not. In my work with people I sought to teach them to examine relentlessly the premises from which they operated in life but I found that the framework of ideas within which they were expected to operate personally was questioned and often vigorously opposed if they questioned certain irrational ideas that were taken for granted. All in all, I found that in my effort to teach openness and honesty, with a respect for independent thinking and compassionate thinking, I was constantly thwarted by dogma and tradition. The newly discovered and more scientific methods of pastoral care were in conflict with more established and traditional ways of seeing people and their behavior. I had the strong feeling that there must be a better theological base to operate from and I sought it. Basically I wanted one that had some of the authority and wisdom of the New Testament, some respect for the traditions that had grown from long human experience, and a compatibility with the insights of contemporary science as far as cosmology, psychology, anthropology and philosophy were concerned. This has been a long step since my father urged me to ask questions and the end result might not be acceptable to him but such is life as it follows its inevitable course.

When I tried to test the rigidity of the church I found that the processes of reason and the thinking that went with reason had little chance against the power of tradition and the vested interests that were tied up in traditional loyalties and persons who saw their futures bound up with the power system. I tested it and found that the church could be tolerant and able to adjust unless it was pressed too far. Then the powers that be swung into action and opposition was ruthlessly swept aside and exile is always the ready answer.

The church played an important part in my education. Some of the things it contributed are deeply ingrained and will always be a part of the essential me. But my education is a never-ending process. I have sought out ways and means of adding interesting skills and insights to my life.

In my efforts to promote my insight into the type of influence that could effect the way other people have thought I had carried on my own educational program which has led to the writing of fifty books and of giving over four thousand lectures. Not all of the books have been printed so I have been the only one to benefit from them. But my efforts to develop some skills in reaching others have paid off. I have had a good life and have been given the chance to contribute to the lives of others and to the process of thinking in my own time. I have been able to do this in spite of the effort of my own church to exclude me from its fellowship but this was limited to a few who used large power for small purposes. The educational process continues and what I have learned from all directions has been a never-ending blessing. What my parents began so well my grandchildren are carrying on in a different time and in a much different way. I am still teaching and counseling and trying as best I can to make a good life possible for as many as possible.

Chapter 5

HEALING AND MYSTICISM

One of the useful dimensions of the mystical awareness is found in the process of healing. I have been fortunate in that I have always enjoyed good health. But during the war I was involved in a crash landing that resulted in a fracture of the top vertebra where the connection is made with the skull. The healing was quite uneventful, though with time a residual condition manifested itself. Pain in the neck was more than just a figure of speech. Also the persistence of a low-grade headache was a fact of life. It was not disabling but it was a nuisance that I would have been glad to get along without. A member of the church I served was a strong believer in both medical and nonmedical forms of healing. After she had spent a weekend with her grandchildren she asked me how I was feeling with an intent look in her eye. I said I felt better but gave no details. For several Sundays she asked the same question until she seemed satisfied that my pains in the neck had disappeared. Then she told me that she had attended a healing service at Mt. Vernon Place Church in Baltimore and had the Worralls place their hands on my atlas vertebra and engage in intersession using her as a surrogate. It seemed to work and I was unaware of what was going on. Then she said she thought I could exert a healing influence too if I tried. With time and preparation that involved study and self-discipline I began having healing services at seven in the morning to accommodate men who usually caught the eight o'clock train for New York City. This early service became a regular event and people came from as far as two hundred miles away to participate. We met fifty two times a year for twelve years and I cannot remember a time when there were not trained medical or nursing personnel in the congregation. That was the service that was never omitted winter or summer and there seemed to be a constant need for whatever there was that people gained from it. This simple service at an ungodly hour seemed to satisfy a need for recognition of a mystical-intuitive quality of life. During much of the time that I was conducting it I was also serving as head of a state-licensed psychiatric clinic with a staff of twenty professionals and sometimes they participated in the service as well. During the twelve years I conducted this service I was unaware of any opposition either to it or the concept that motivated it. I am quite sure that I laid on hands for healing over forty thousand times and no one had any ill effects though many claimed beneficial effects therefrom.

It was a service that gave free rein to the intuitive-mystical feelings that might have been present in the minds and spirits of the persons participating. Everything was low key. The service had no publicity. No one was urged to attend. No one was thanked for coming. I certainly never claimed to be a healer. All I ever claimed for anyone was a strong belief in the wonder of the human spirit and its mystical nature. Nothing more needed to be claimed to allow full play of the mystical nature. This starting point for an active interest in the healing impulse had many ramifications. Although we never allowed articles to be written calling attention to the program I was asked often to speak about it. It was always done in a low key manner with no claims and with the idea that if the spirit is recognized and given a chance to manifest itself nobody needs to claim anything, for it will show itself.

It was about this time that I met Dr. Lawrence LeShan through his wife whom I had hired to run our adult education program in the psychiatric clinic already mentioned. He was a clinical and research psychologist primarily interested in the study of cancer. He found that in his study of the etiology of cancer almost invariably the onset followed a major traumatic event usually in a time frame of from six months to two years. But he found that as he pursued his study he was blocked by pathologists who did not approve of his research. It was about this time that I became interested in his work. We teamed up to explore cancer from a somewhat different stance from the cancer organizations that were most well known and financially supported. We have continued our studies and have published our findings in books, professional journals and more popular journals. Yet the impact of our studies did not seem to get much attention. The three accepted forms of cancer treatment involved body assaultive methods, radiation, chemotherapy and surgery. The methods that we recommended were not used generally because they seemed to have involved less research and did not seem to have as spectacular results. They were; psychotherapy, which aimed to change the emotional content of consciousness, another non-assaultive method referred to as immunotherapy, and the third method, most akin to mysticism, spiritual therapy. These methods are old and yet new for they have been neglected in recent years but are being rediscovered by physicians themselves. Research has found that the three non-assaultive methods were used during the middle of the last century, perhaps in modified forms, because there was no other method. With the dramatic improvements in surgery more spectacular results were achieved by removing the offending tissue. Soon after in the early part of this century there were major developments in chemotherapy and radiation therapy. The non-assaultive methods took a back seat and those who interpret research findings look with misgivings on the alleged progress we have made. We feel that there may be some value in trying to understand the forces that are a part of the healing process. At this point some of my attitudes have been a detriment to some perceptive scientific stance. I had the feeling for years that I was merely an instrument in the hands of God and that it was not important for me to understand the process by which healing took place. I made no effort to keep records or check up on the results. I had the idea that too much interest in the mechanics of the process would lead to the loss of the ability I might have.

So for years I made no effort to keep track of what happened. I assumed that the process was beyond my understanding and that too much interest in the details would destroy any ability I contributed to the process. In more recent years I have revised my thinking about the whole process and especially my own part in it. I have come to assume that I am an active contributor to whatever it is that proves to be efficacious. I have gone over in my mind the things that have occurred and I will try to record them as I recall them without trying to interpret what happened and why. In that way we may gain some insight into dynamic factors that may have been operative. I will give as brief an account of what happened as possible with a thought that it should be sufficient to give some clues as to the dynamics involved. I pick these cases of a much larger sampling that would be possible. The first case involved a couple who were not actively engaged in any of the special services designed to give expression to any mystical awareness. Mr. D. was troubled with blinding migraine headaches that had persisted for years and just about ruined one day a week. He was a Parisian dress designer who had come to New York to work in the women's clothing industry. He was Jewish and his wife was English with membership in our church. She was not a regular attendant but had some knowledge of parish activities. This morning she told her husband he should go to church and get rid of his headache. He staggered to the church on his own for this first time. He stood in the back for a while to get his bearings and then walked to the front of the sanctuary. When it came time for the laying on of hands he took his place kneeling at the altar with several others. After the service he went to the railroad station with some of the other men. I had no chance to speak with him. That evening the doorbell rang while I was eating dinner with my family. Mr. D. was standing there and he asked one question without hesitation. He asked," What did you do to me this morning?" I asked him in and said he was there and knew what was done and I asked why he wanted to know. He said it was one of the strangest days he had ever had for he should have had a severe migraine but he didn't have any. He said that he couldn't understand what had happened to him. We talked about what had happened to him. He has never had another migraine and I still hear from him on occasion. Without any urging he joined the church, a men's spiritual life study group and went through quite a life change. He evidently had quite a mystical experience on his own terms and spent years reading and studying the meaning of his experience and would tell you if you asked that it was one of the most important events that ever happened to him.

Quite a different kind of a case involved Mrs. G. who had been an active member of the church, singing in the choir for years. She had not been in attendance for weeks and we had heard nothing from her. I was told that she had a severe dermatitis and was miserable. I went to her home and she admitted me and presented a sight of human misery. Her legs and arms were covered with lesions. These were superating and gave an ugly appearance. She said that now I could tell why she had missed church. She said this had been coming on for some months but for a long time it didn't show, but now it had gotten worse. At the local supermarket they had asked her not to shop there any more because there had been complaints from customers about her touching the fruits. She said she had been doctoring for months but just got worse. Her family found it difficult to touch her and she said she felt like she had leprosy. I asked if she minded if I engaged in the discipline of prayer on her be-half. She said of course not. So I placed one hand on her forehead and the other gently on the lesions that covered her forearm and remained

46

in silent prayer for several minutes. Then before I left I assured her that I would be back in a week or so. But before I could get back her dermatologist called and said she wanted to see me at once. I agreed and before long this woman physician I knew quite well and admired for her skill as a physician was confronting me with accusations of practicing medicine without proper authorization. We talked for a while about the areas where our interests might overlay. Then she said that she had been treating Mrs. G. for six months and she got worse until the week when she reported my visit and the dramatic improvement. She said the lesions were cleared up and were only marked by red spots. The patient reported feeling much better. Then the dermatologist talked seriously about what we thought had happened and why. I believe she learned to have a new respect for the role of the spiritual therapist as we talked that morning. Mrs. G. appeared to be completely cured of her skin problem within a couple of weeks and was again singing in the choir. The dynamic factors in her case were obviously quite different from those in the case previously reviewed. They were both dealing with important suffering from social and emotional problems. Important psychosomatic problems could have been involved.

Another case involved Mr. and Mrs. S. She was the intake social worker at the psychiatric center I headed up. Her husband was a concert pianist with the Columbia Artists Bureau. I knew them quite well in a professional role. He had a heart attack and was rushed to a cardiologist who did extensive testing and ordered him to cut his activities to a minimum. In addition to his occasional concerts he was carrying a heavy load of teaching of piano pupils. They had just bought an expensive new home and his illness placed them in financial straits. Although they were both Jewish and had never shown any interest in religious things, Mrs. S. said to her husband "Why don't you go to see Dr. Jackson. He does strange things to people." When he came we talked quite earnestly for nearly an hour about his feelings and attitude of mind. Then I asked him if he minded if I stood behind his chair with my hands upon his shoulders. He raised no objection so I did a laying on of hands for five minutes or so. He jumped to his feet and asked what I had done for it felt like electric currents going through his body. We talked about his feelings and then I recommended that he return immediately to his cardiologist and have another reading. He did and the doctor said he had a completely different reading. He reported a normal heart action and recommended that he cut his teaching back to a less burdensome level and come back in two weeks for another test. Mr. and Mrs. S. were much pleased with the turn of events and Mr. S. if he would meet me on the street would be loudly effusive in his praise of me as his healer even though I never made such a claim. They began coming to church with their two children and seemed to find a new meaning in life. The stabilized condition in his life seemed to remain for years and there were no further heart attacks to my knowledge. This was quite different from the previous two cases but in all of them there was a role of an authority figure who might have exerted influence.

One day a phone call came from another pastor who lived about seventy-five miles further up the New Haven railroad line. He told me about a case of a woman in his town who was suicidal. He said he did not feel comfortable seeing her anymore and wondered if I would be willing to see her. She had a disfiguring operation for cancer and was scheduled for further treatment at Memorial hospital. The Sloan Kettering Research Laboratory was located in our town so I made inquiry concerning her at the hospital and also at the research facility. She concurred in the story the pastor had told. She was scheduled for tests in about two weeks. We made plans to meet her at the train station in a few days. She arrived on schedule and I found her to be a deeply angry woman who resented me, her husband, her parents, in fact everyone. The only bright spot I found was in the fact that she had come. She wanted none of my faith and said I must be crazy to believe such rubbish. In a two and a half hour session, I tried to draw out all the anger I could, and it was considerable. The hospital had found nodes that they planned to excise. She wanted none of it and again repeated her suicidal threats. I accepted her feelings and did not argue with her. We traced the roots of her feelings and shared her thoughts as far as possible without affirming her negations. She poured out her anger and resentment endlessly. When I told her a prayer group specially trained in intercession would adopt her if she were willing. She expressed hostility saying that if they were stupid enough to believe such garbage let them do what they would. By the time she was ready to catch her return train she was limp from the emotional exertion of pouring out hostility and resentment. But she agreed to come again after she had the examination at the hospital. In the meantime I had followed her progress at the hospital and talked with some of the physicians that were related to the case. They reported that careful examination did not reveal the nodes they expected to find. She was quite a changed person when she returned next time. She was more mellow and less resentful and agreed that what we were doing might be of some value. We had several more sessions before I returned her to her pastor's care. She kept going to the hospital but on a less demanding schedule. She has not had the second operation. She made peace with her family and joined the church she had ridiculed and became a leader of a prayer group. I still hear from her occasionally and she has had no further treatment for cancer. One event that had quite an effect on her was the time we went to the church alone for the laying on of hands in silence and the tears ran freely down her cheeks.

During the weeks that we worked together we treated more than her physical condition. As she gave up her hatred her body was more at peace with herself and showed it. Working with people toward health is hard work and takes the best that is in one.

A case of an industrialist who was my friend was quite different in its demands upon me. He loved surfcasting and was engaging in his favorite sport when he injured his knee. He didn't know how it happened. He could not unbend his knee. He crawled to shore and with difficulty drove to the nearest doctor who could not get his leg unbound. Then he went to the emergency room of the nearest hospital where it seemed they were unable to do anything to help him. They were able to ease the pain temporarily while he moved to a Veterans Hospital where they scheduled an operation for the next morning. I hastened to call on my friend with no intention of interfering with his treatment. He still hadn't been able to unlock the knee joint. While visiting with him in his room I asked if he would mind if I tried something. He was willing so I placed one hand about four inches below the locked joint and the other about the same distance above it. I was quiet as I went into the altered state of consciousness usually employed at such times and remained in a prayerful mood. After several minutes I took my hands away and noticed the surprised look on his face. He moved his knee freely back and forth and said for the first time since this happened, "I am free of pain". He left the hospital within the hour and had no recurrence of the difficulty since. He stopped to see me after returning from the winter in Florida. He is convinced there was a miracle involved but I argue against it. I don't believe in miracles for they violate my idea of the structure of the universe. I want a dependable God not a capricious being who is moved by the whims or importuning of mortals. In fact the whole idea turns me off as childish and unworthy of a rational adult. However I can understand a mystical frame of mind that moves beyond the usual way of looking at things to understand the unusual possibilities of human consciousness. This is often observed in cases of acute pain.

Estelle, my wife, was a case in point. I was away speaking on Prince Edward Island. Estelle thought she would surprise me by mowing the lawn. She slipped on a bank and twisted her ankle so that it broke in four places. Being alone she crawled into the house with her foot dangling and called my brother who took her to the Health Center. After x-rays it was decided that she must go to Mary Hitchcock Hospital connected with Dartmouth Medical Center. The next morning they operated as I winged my way homeward. My daughter Lois met me at the airport and we were waiting in the room when Estelle was brought down from the recovery room. She complained of acute and unbearable pain in the ankle. She wanted us to call the doctor to remove the cast immediately. We felt that was not practical so we reverted to the next possibility. I asked my daughter to go around the bed and take hold of my wife's hand and place her other hand on her forehead. I placed my hands upon the cast near the incisions on her ankle. We held them there for five minutes or so and by that time Estelle was in a deep sleep. When she awakened there was no pain. In the three months that followed with three different casts there was no occasion of pain and there was no discomfort. The doctors at Mary Hitchcock did a skillful job and the healing was perfect and uneventful. She is again mowing the lawn, which she claims she enjoys.

Another friend of ours is totally blind but lets her handicap interfere with life as little as possible. She was walking on a street in Washington, D.C. when she fell from the curb and broke her leg just below the knee. After a brief hospital stay she returned home and had considerable pain. She had it looked at in the hospital, but the discomfort persisted. I spent some time with her and tried to help with the knee and leg. The laying on of hands was efficacious and she has no further pain although the doctors say they cannot understand it because the bones have obviously knitted unevenly. The pain or discomfort has been explained in more detail in the chapter on mysticism and pain.

Another case of pain is that of F.S. who has been a friend of ours more than a half century. She hobbled around with painful arthritis. I did a laying on of hands and the pain was much better. A second laying on of hands completed the process of removing the pain. She says that it is largely nonexistent now but each year while she occupies our guesthouse she requests a booster shot, which is insurance for another year.

A further case is interesting as he is a physician with advanced degrees in both psychology and physics. He had been troubled for four years by acute lower back pain. He had tried every type of physician and therapy that had been suggested to him. None were affective and he had become resigned to his painful and disabling state. He slept on a board. He could not carry even a brief case and when he traveled he engaged porters to carry everything. He was a young man in his thirties with an active professional life that was impaired by his physical condition. I first met him at a conference of professionals interested in human consciousness in Iceland. His specialty was in the designing and development of very sensitive measuring devices for the electrical currents of molecules and other infinitesimal sources of energy. He came to me on the third day of the weeklong conference and said he understood that I had a strange power over people and he laughed. Then he told me of his condition and wondered if I would be willing to try it with him. With a sort of apologetic aside he said nothing else had worked. I asked him to meet me in a vacant third floor room at four that afternoon when the conference sessions were over. We sat down together and talked about the subtle energies that were present everywhere in nature. Then we talked about the marvelous energies of consciousness. He went right along with it for this was his field. Then I explained about the laying on of hands and the energies that were transferred thereby. He understood. Then after about an hour of this I asked if he was ready for the laying on of hands and he was. I stood behind his chair placing my hands on his shoulders just over the ganglia that controlled the main nerve supply to either side of his body. I kept my hands there for five or ten minutes while I was in an altered state of consciousness. Then I said, "That's it". He got up slowly and moved his body about tentatively. Then he started bending at the waist and after several tries touched his feet with the comment that he hadn't done that for years. On Saturday morning when I took my bags down to be stowed on the bus there was our scientist throwing bags up to the bus driver on top of the bus stowing them away. When I cautioned him about such strenuous activity, he responded by quoting scripture, "O ye of little faith". Two years later I had a phone call from a dean at the University of Vermont asking if I would co-teach a course in their summer school with a physicist named Buryl Payne for he said he would not come unless I came with him. We had a good time together and his back was in excellent condition.

The next case was centered in a hospital where I was working, not as a physician but teaching crisis management. I was there in that capacity for ten years. A patient was brought to me to see what I could do with her as she was considered a risk for surgery as she had a calcium spur in her neck where the tolerances for surgery were too risky. She could not move her neck and held her head in a stiff position with rigid control for if she didn't the pain was acute. She wore a surgical collar at night. I talked with her for nearly an hour preparing her for my type of intervention. She was a religious person and was willing to cooperate. When it came time for the laying on of hands I held one hand on her forehead and the other on the back of her neck over the place where the calcium spur was located. In silence I held that position for five or ten minutes until it felt right to move them. Then I said that is all there is to it. She moved tentatively for a minute or two and then more vigorously up and down and from left to right. There seemed to be no impediment to her movement and her attendant said it looked as if the spur had been dissolved. She left feeling quite elated and has remained so. This spring after the lapse of several years she reported no recurrence. It is a matter of the hospital records and Ray Stephens the chaplain at the time says he will verify the process on request. The hospital staff shake their heads at the mention of the case for it seems to be out of their department except to verify their observations.

Perhaps we have space for one more case a bit different from the rest. I was giving a series of lectures on science and religion for the California Conference of the Congregational church. One of the ten lectures was on health and healing. Two people came up when the conference was over to say thanks and incidentally they asked if I thought I could help their daughter. I said I never knew what would happen because it was in the hands of God and I was only an instrument. So we made an appointment for Sunday afternoon at a church in San Francisco.

The details as I learned them were that their daughter Megan had been riding in a car that was hit head on by a drunk driver. The car was set on fire and she was not able to get out. The young man sought help and the fire spread. She tried to protect her eyes but by the time help came she had been severely burned about the face, neck and arms. She was hospitalized and had extensive plastic surgery. She also suffered great damage to her self-esteem for her appearance caused people who saw her to gasp and look aghast. When I first saw her I had difficulty in keeping from showing my reaction to her scarred face. I asked her father and mother and her two sisters to sit within reach of her while I stood in the pew behind her. Being a minister's family they were acquainted with the procedures. Starting with her neck and gradually moving up to her chin and face on to her forehead and continuing this process in a altered state of consciousness for about an hour with no spoken word. At the end of the hour we parted and I did not see any of them for a year. At a seminar at a Presbyterian church in a suburb of San Francisco I entered the auditorium and as I spoke was drawn to an attractive young woman who sat in the second row who smiled broadly. Another more mature woman in the back was also grinning broadly and seemed to know me even though I did not place her. At the morning's break both of the women came toward me. When I saw them together I remembered them as the young woman with the sadly disfigured face and her mother. I said " You must have had lots of plastic surgery since I saw you last." She said that no one had touched her face since that Sunday afternoon when I first saw her. She has also had a complete revival of her spirit and is a delight to be around. While the plastic surgeons deserve most of the credit for her restoration I think her family and their faith deserve commendation for their loving support and their belief in the spiritual power to heal. She has come to our farm home in Vermont to spend some time letting us share the buoyancy of her spirit.

I think I have given a fair sample of the way I see the healing process shown in the encounters I have had with all types of people under all types of circumstances. They represent a tiny fraction of those people that I have encountered during the last thirty years or so. I have given very little interpretation of my philosophy of healing, just a brief overview of how the mystical perception reflects itself in the healing experience of persons. In the next chapter I will try to give more of my own feeling about what takes place and what the possibilities and shortcomings may be.

Chapter 6

THE SCIENTIST AS MYSTIC

My aunt Dorothy played an important part in my education from an early age. By the time I was nine years of age I was spending a large part of each day at the biological lab and the eugenics record office of the Carnegie Institute where she was engaged as a research assistant. With infinite patience in answering the myriad questions a wide-eyed youngster could ask, and not having had any children of her own, she made a large place in her life for me. I was allowed to play with the white mice and rats and seemed never to tire of watching these little creatures that I was led to believe were contributing so nobly to scientific exploration. She performed thousands of operations splicing cancer cells into healthy tissue so that its development could be observed. The high point in her life seemed to be the time one of her experiments was accepted and printed in "Science". I looked forward to vacation time for I was then able to work with her.

On days off from the lab my aunt's searches did not end. Then we would travel the fields and streams to explore the wonders of life as nature revealed it. One day with our tools of discovery in hand we wandered across the fields until we came to a pond that looked like a large puddle. Yet before the day was over it had become a place of wonder. I learned about whirligigs, water spiders and many other fabulous creatures that could do wonderful things on the surface of the water. Then we used our nets to look into the water and out came many forms of life, little fish and turtles, little crawling things and others that got away after giving us glimpses of the wonder. After asking if I thought anything lived in the mud she dug up a scoop of blackish substance and began to carefully examine it. It proved to be very much alive and we remained fascinated with our find for a long time. We found minute shells like little clams or mussels. We found a special kind of worm. We recognized the skeletons of leaves and flowers that had grown around the pond and now were a part of the mud. We came to realize how even a handful of seemingly valueless mud could be a place of awe and wonder when you looked at it in the right way.

I came to be a person with special privilege about the lab. I realized that important work was going on around there so I was never to interfere. And nothing was to interrupt the work or distract attention from the work at hand for often it was a matter of life and death, even if it was of a little creature who was giving all for science. I didn't know how dangerous the research might be until one day quite a bit later people began talking in guarded ways and I sensed that something was wrong. When I had a chance with my Aunt alone I asked what was the matter when everyone went around whispering and always talking about C. She said probably they did not understand how well I understood things. She said there was a kind of animal cancer that was quite rare among people, and that some way or other she had contracted some of it but that they were working on it and hoped to be successful. We agreed not to say anything about this to other people and she would keep me informed of developments. She was true to her promise and she and I took that part of my education seriously. She won the battle against anthrax and had two other kinds of cancer before she died at the ripe age of 82. My aunt gave me a rich and meaningful introduction to science that was the bedrock on which later experience was built. She personalized and humanized scientific study in a way that books and lectures could never do. My years in high school gave flesh to the informal study in the lab and the structure that began to emerge was to become a permanent part of my life.

A few years later my aunt married Dr. Hugo Fricke who had been for years Nils Bohr's first assistant in the Institute in Copenhagen. Because of the brilliance of his mind he was sent to the Carnegie Institute to coordinate the research and study that engaged them. Because of the union with my aunt and the American scientific community he never again returned to his native land except for visits. One of the privileges of my life has been to spend long evenings at their home on the Institute grounds in Cold Spring Harbor. His research and study has for many decades contributed to my understanding of the scientific developments of the period.

After scouting universities at Princeton, Cornell and comparable schools, for financial and family reasons I decided on Ohio Wesleyan. My years in college were significant for me. I decided to do major studies in Geology. This was a basic science essential to understanding some of the social and theological issues prevalent in the period of the 1930's. I found some answers that have stayed with me for the rest of my life. Yet they did not satisfy my philosophical quest and I changed my major in my senior year to studies that would lead to special interest in discovering meanings rather than methods of knowing. This led me to two years of theological study at Drew University. While valuable in showing where we had come from it was disappointing in throwing light on where we were going. It was like taking a trip back to the Middle Ages and had the lingering flavor of musty things.

So I went to Union Theological Seminary in the Columbia orbit. A year spent there was rewarding for the chance to study with Reinhold Neibuhr, Harry Ward, Eugene Lyman, Paul Tillich and Harry Emerson Fosdick. But while the professors were brilliant the general atmosphere seemed to lack a quality of integration. So I journeyed on to New Haven for three years further study which was most useful for me for I was allowed to supplement my studies with work at the School of Human Relations at Yale as their school of personality studies was then called. Here I was able to pursue my studies of human beings and all of the concerns that were relevant to human processes. Studies that were important then have remained central to my thinking for half a century and were important to the development of my main therapeutic explorations in the years that followed.

At Yale I gave myself to two fields of study, psychology and communication. The first was a scientific study of behavior and the second was a communication of ideas with clarity and precision. During the decade of the thirties financing graduate studies was a problem but at Yale I had maximum opportunity with minimum financial burden. It was there that I first heard of Henry Margenau, a distinguished professor of physics. With time he became an important figure in my effort to bring compatibility to my studies of mind and behavior.

Further studies in the nature and understanding of personality were the natural outgrowth of my three years at Yale so I decided on more work in the understanding of human personality. Three more years at the Postgraduate Center of Psychotherapy studying psychotherapeutics, psychodynamics and psychoneuroses helped to fill in some of the blank spots in my education but they introduced me to a life long study in these fields of interest. In this eclectic school I found that the study of human beings was a varied and extensive experience of learning and it touched every aspect of my original interest in religion and the search for truth. Further the Center introduced me to a faculty with broad experience in professional interests. From school with an explicit interest in religion

I was now the only such person in a body of two hundred plus professionals given to the study and treatment of human beings who were having trouble experiencing life. Religion was treated as behavior and not usually of the healthy type. I was usually treated as exhibit A and that experience forced me to a new level of understanding of myself and others. My increasing study and publication in the behavioral studies caused me to have a widening circle of those doing studies in related areas. So I was invited to share in professional conferences about the world, at home in the States as well as in such out of the way places as Iceland and Majorca.

Some time after my Iceland experience I was invited to spend ten days with a group of personality scientists and physicists on the Island of Majorca. They were to be carefully selected from Europe and North America and were to be invited to this all-expenses-paid gathering because of what they could contribute based on their own studies. The participants were to be limited to a dozen and were to meet without agenda for a free exchange of ideas concerning the nature and use of energy as the basic force in physical and spiritual life. It was an effort to get behind all of the presuppositions that were taken for granted in contemporary scientific research. We were told not to prepare papers or other items that would stand in the way of complete spontaneity. We were isolated in an ancient castle about three miles outside of the main city on the island. The surroundings were ideal for an exploration such as ours. We were meeting in the library of the castle in the midst of thousands of ancient books. We could not be unaware of our encompassing climate of thought and feeling. Mrs. Margenau came to me that afternoon and said she was worried about Henry and she described his insomnia. I called Dr. LeShan and we talked over a plan of action concerning Henry Margenau. Dr. LeShan and I had the rooms on either side of the Margenaus. We told Mrs. Margenau not to say anything to her husband but that beginning an hour after they had retired we would begin thinking strong thoughts of deep relaxation and sleep. Next morning she said that he had had the best nights sleep in a long time. So we continued the thoughts of relaxation every other night with the result that he reported good sleep every other night and was rather mystified by the experience. We thought about Henry Margenau's experience in relation to the influence of minute and quite unmeasurable charges of electricity and our thinking led to more experimentation later.

The conference led us into quite plausible ideas that we could not credit with scientific accuracy but were well within the realm of scientific validity. Among our group of scientifically oriented individuals there was agreement that our time together was indeed valuable at the point where we allowed our conjecturing to run free of the usual scientific restraints imposed by our subservience to the methodology of scientific research and our fear of our unbridled consciousness. We tried to develop ways of penetrating the barriers so that the creativity of our minds was not bridled by our habitual mode of thinking. We left Majorca with a determination to work to free our minds from our self-imposed restraints. Dr. Margenau and Dr. LeShan agreed to work on a book that would see if there were room at the interface of physics and psychology to maneuver and develop some valid way of looking at the phenomena of that development. We found that our time together had set our minds free to think in new channels and we were enriched by the experience even though we did not have substantive claims of important breakthroughs. We found a euphoria in our free exchange of thought and feeling.

Several months went by with no significant communication between the participants in the Majorca conference. My wife and I were taking some time to relax and study on Sanibel Island in the Gulf of Mexico when I received an urgent telephone call from Dr. LeShan asking for assistance in a special project to test in more detail the theses we had looked at tentatively in our work with Dr. Margenau and his insomnia in Majorca. He outlined how we would proceed to make our procedure free of any outside interference. He said Henry's insomnia had gotten so bad that he was going to a specialist to try for help. He was to keep a detailed record of his wakefulness and sleeping for a month. My part was to keep an equally careful record of my quiet meditation about him during this period, which was to be determined by a random selection of dates of which no one had knowledge except me. He said to take a phone book, open it at random, and beginning with the lower right hand corner count up the first three digits in order until I had a month's worth. Then he said to follow that order as I had copied from the phone book, for instance if the first number was 2 and the second was 3 meditate on Henry's peace of mind on the 2nd night and then skip two nights so that the second session would be on the third night and so on for the month. Henry was in New Haven, LeShan in New York and I on an island in the Gulf of Mexico. After asking questions about procedure I agreed to be on duty every night that was specified by our code at 10 p.m. The effort was to affect a change of consciousness for about fifteen minutes during which time Henry Margenau was held in focus. I worked out my series of dates and performed as requested. Neither Henry nor his doctor knew anything about our efforts. We felt that this would give to our effort the effect of a double blind psychic experiment. It was not until the doctor and Henry had completed their evaluation of the month's dates that Dr. LeShan went to New Haven and explained our effort and asked to be able to compare the record the doctor kept with the record I kept in the Gulf of Mexico. We found that there was a significant correlation and I have the letter from Henry Margenau thanking me for my efforts in his behalf. It seemed that in this simple experiment we had tentatively shown that some form of energy could be transferred to be effective without a conscious awareness and over a considerable distance. We were prepared now to continue our experimentation with a more extensive effort. We were now in a position to look at phenomena such as extrasensory communication and even intercessory prayer in a different light.

Many of the things that had been observed from time past were now seen not as miracles but as the operations of minute charges of energy following their own laws with predictable results. It will have to be followed out with many and more precise testing, but it may indicate new directions for our explanation of phenomena of thought and subtle action.

Sir John Eccles and Lord Adrian have been following the earlier suggestion of Sir. Wm. Cecil Dampier Wetham that the researches in science might lead to more spiritual discoveries in time. Human exploration of consciousness may open doors of exploration that will make it possible to see meanings and relationships that we are just beginning to understand. These explorations may open the way for approaches to many fields of science where mystery seems to lead to greater mystery. The missing element in the puzzle of creation may be closer to our understanding than we have comprehended. All of this makes the wonder and mystery of the self seem to be an ever more inviting area of research than we have thought in the past. All of this throws new light on the perception of the mystic who believes that the researches of science have a depth dimension that points the way beyond the impasses of materialistic research.

One day recently while my wife and I were taking some courses at Oxford I was as usual searching the rare book section of Blackwell's. A recent purchase of books was spread out on a couple of tables of books. Some scholar of mysticism had apparently died and his library was turned over to Blackwell's for sale. I saw at once that I must have about fifty of the volumes related to mysticism, to science and philosophy. My wife was looking at another section of Blackwell's extensive basement. We had a thousand dollars held in reserve in case of emergency. I called my wife, reported an emergency, and soon we were engaged in shipping cartons of books to our Vermont home. Here was a treasure house of scholarly books, many of them long out of print, which deals with the effort to understand that subterranean realm where science and philosophy move out beyond their depths of understanding and point to the insight the mystic discerns just beyond the boundaries of his lucid perception but within the reach of his vital imagination.

I sit alone in my study in the Vermont hills thinking of what science has accomplished in this century. I think of my Aunt Dorothy and her love of research into the mysteries of cancer and its baffling impact on life. I think of the nights I talked with my Uncle Hugo after he had taken over the Fermi experiments at the Argonnne Laboratories as he pondered the question of life and death and human fate. I think of the human disappointment of his life who saw his hope for physical immortality through children stolen from him by the invisible energy of the x-ray tube, and raising the question about the other forms of survival hinted at by his scientific surmise of indestructibility. Was his conscious mind playing a trick on him in holding before him an idea of a spiritual dimension held apart from all of the rest of creation? If everything else in creation changes form but is not destroyed, then he asked, should human consciousness be singled out for destruction when it gives meaning to all the rest? I thought of all those who were holding on to life because of his discoveries in the fight with cancer when his own body seemed helpless against its ravages. The self-sacrificing quality of science's search for truth was evidenced by something more that both impelled that search and revealed the mystical quest for a truth that was larger than dogma for it shared the size of life itself.

My Aunt Dorothy had a love for science that was larger than life. She in her own unique way transmitted it to me. Others have wittingly or unwittingly added to this vision of truth. Some like the religious fundamentalists have been so afraid of the great truth that they have concocted all manner of falsehoods to avoid looking at it full in the face. They have been satisfied with a little vision-and suffer the consequences. Others have stood in awe of the splendor of creation and sought out its secrets with respect.

I early realized that there are two types of scientists separated one from the other by qualities of personality. There are those who let their lives be bounded by measurements and observations of the phenomena that are external and can be quantified. The others tread the boundaries of awe and wonder with the mood of expectancy. They too are concerned about observations but they are always looking beyond what they see with their eyes. They are more truly contemplative as if everything has another and more significant dimension that is just beyond reach.

Mysticism is sometimes misunderstood as a nonrational process of the emotions. This is a mistaken concept for while the emotions are clearly involved the mystical experience appears to be an integrative process in which mind, emotion, physiological endowment as well as cumulative perception are melded into a transcendent form of understanding supplemented by heightened awareness of relationships and meanings. The scientist-mystic brings together the energies of consciousness and the inventive-creative capacities of the mind in a way that makes something new—something that has not existed before.

I have gone through a long and interesting life and have had many interesting encounters with scientists. I have evaluated each of them to see if they have approached their work with the sense of awe and wonder that my Aunt Dorothy reflected. If they did not have it they might be sincere and industrious but I had the feeling that something was lacking. I felt sorry for them because they were missing an important part of the scientist's experience. Maybe it was because Dorothy means lover of God and the truly scientific soul is always looking for the deeper meanings of life with its many varied experiences. The mystic's perception adds much to the meaning of life and the role of the scientist would be filled with an unusual burden if there were no meaning to research.

The scientific method provides opportunities for great moments of discovery. I have enjoyed what little I have been able to share of that encounter with the growing edge of human exploration. My Aunt Dorothy has been but a part of that gift to modern life that has been contributed by the scientific spirit.

Science has a way of becoming a religion for some followers of the limited method employed. This comes about without a full awareness of what is involved in the process. Science follows a precise set of rubrics as if it were committed to a religious conviction without realizing that there is something incompatible about that behavior. The scientist moves beyond his normal frame of reference when he considers things that are not bound by measurements of space and time. As science pushes out the boundaries of its explorations it begins to encounter a no-mans land where the traditional province of the two contending forces become entwined. The scientific study of religion runs into similar difficulties as it tries to put limits on those things that are not easily reduced to measurements. It seems as if some language such as that the mystic uses serves a valid purpose in bridging the gap between the purely measuremental and the direction in which it points. In his best thinking the scientist is always just a short step away from the metaphysical but that seems to be a step he cannot take without violating a major commitment. For instance Howard Gardner in his book Frames of Mind talks about the dilemma of the scientist in more mature years who seeks to find in metaphysics a brand of reality that is never found in pure science alone. He resists the inclination of the maturing mind to move beyond a limiting frame of reference to find more space to expand his more reasoned accumulation of judgment and experience. He apparently has not paid attention to the admonition of Max Planck who pointed out that the scientist cannot help becoming a metaphysician when he asks the question "why" for meaning always moves beyond the simple measurement that is the realm of pure science. When the "how" is compromised by the "why" a major change in direction is implied.

Chapter 7

THE ARTIST AS MYSTIC

My brother was an artist. I have watched him develop since early childhood. He would always use a visual symbol rather than a verbal symbol for after all that is what a word is. Even in the earliest days there were advantages to the graphic symbol. When we attended church we were cautioned not to talk but my brother was encouraged to illustrate the homilies. Through the years he used graphic forms to show what was going on in his inner world. He used different types of graphic expression in the varied forms of childhood expression just as he went through various art forms to express the moods of adult mental and emotional activity. When he was a student in a school of art and architecture he used forms that gave expression to architectonic perceptions. Then he became primarily interested in people and gave himself to portraiture. This was followed by a period of philosophical abstraction and the graphic forms employed showed the effect of his thinking. Then came a period of mathematical abstraction with the graphic forms that gave expression to this thought process.

Now that he has spent a lifetime teaching students the rudiments of artistic understanding and was able to settle back in retirement to do what he really wanted to do he looked away from his mountain retreat with quite a different perspective on life and art. Some of his artwork shows this more philosophical perspective. His art has always been an expression of what has been going on deep within but it has always been filtered through a form of mystical knowing.

The use of words has always seemed to be misleading and partial. I remember asking him what a painting meant and he seemed frustrated for if he had not made himself known through the medium of his art he certainly would not be able to succeed better by reducing his thought and feeling to what he considered a less exacting form of communication, mere words. He warned against the temptation of reducing meaning by changing the form of expression to a more familiar though less exacting form of expression. He would recommend study of a medium until it became a valid form for expressing an idea or a feeling. He explained the variety of forms of expressing graphic art. There is portraiture, to study people. There is landscape to study and appreciate the earth. There is caricature to bring ridicule, humor to show human foibles. Still life can show the detail of a flower or a human creation. A poetic image can stimulate a deeper perception just as a likeness can give you a chance to see someone with clearer understanding.

An abstraction can bring to life a perception that might easily be missed in a verbal illustration. My daughter was the medical illustrator on the faculty of a medical school where one of her tasks was to make clear by graphic illustration physical relationships that might not be easily perceived in life. A painting may be used to make clear the dramatic force of a historical or personal event. A map may be a work of art as it produces a world of relationships. There was a time when few people could read, when the people were taught the great spiritual truths by church windows that told the stories of sacred literature and gargoyles acted out in stone the stories that were easily accessible to the multitudes.

Audubon had the mystical awareness of a naturalist and communicated his vision so that humans ever after saw the wonderful creation he saw in the world of birds. The great men of the past live in the reality of their images caught by artists. The Mona Lisa caught the mystery of women for all time. Beauty and ugliness are revealed in their deeper meanings as the artist portrays them. The imaginings of the fantastic are preserved in the paintings of the artist's creations as they are kept alive in the great works of fiction.

The beginnings and the ends of life are preserved by those artists who penetrate the meanings of birth and death. Biography and portraits keep alive the memories of those who made their lives memorable. The saints and the sinners of the past have left the marks on those who came after them by the mystical means that were captured by the vivid portrayals of artists known and unknown. And each has been able to say something beyond words that would have been lost forever without the visions that were put into a less transitory form by their talent.

Humanity seems to have had a deep need to see more than is easily put into words so that it may become a part of that treasured revelation that each age passes on to the next. The sculptors of Greece and Rome and the painters of the Renaissance, the architects of the cathedrals and those who told their stories in glass were all paying tribute to something beyond their art that had a right to live after them. This is so characteristic of the mystics who are so aware of another dimension of creation that they want to hold on to and preserve for those who come after them. The artists are the mystics of all ages who see so clearly what came before them and what will come after them and they want to keep alive the vital link that gives meaning to the human experience.

Perhaps most of those who are influenced by artists do not realize that they are feeling the power of the artists to create the mystical awareness. Because it is so difficult to define, it often comes about without a precise characterization. When you stand before a painting you are charged with an energy that is part of the experience but is not limited by what is in you or the picture. It is something new that emerges from the encounter. Perhaps we can best illustrate the happening by using a couple of artists to show how it happens.

I once was invited to visit the private chapel on the estate of John Carroll who was a signer of the Declaration of Independence from the State of Maryland. I did not know what was in the chapel. Yet I gave an exclamation and said I did not know that two such exquisite El Grecos were to be found in this country outside of museums. The tradition of the family had been to give as little publicity to the rare possession as possible. The tradition of the family for two hundred years was to keep this spiritual treasure to themselves. It did something to them and for them that was so personal that they did not want it to become commonplace. Perhaps that is one of the special meanings of a treasured art object, that it lights the way to a mystical illumination. Perhaps that is one of the special values of a great artist like El Greco. I have beaten a pathway not only to the treasures of Toledo and Madrid but to many of the El Grecos I have been able to find in the collections of the world. As I have been able to stand before the work of this Greek-Italian-Spanish artist with his strangely elongated figures I have felt deeply moved. I have returned in thought to Iraklion to try to understand what drove the artist. I have searched the streets and museums of Florence and Rome thinking that I might ferret out the mystical awareness that possessed the artist's consciousness. I have stood in awe within the walls of Padua. I have sought out the intimacy of his home in Toledo as well as the collection of saints in the Cathedral in the same hill town, and always I share the dual experience of being both satisfied and unsatisfied. Perhaps that is always the experience as one is ushered into the mystery of mystical awareness. There is the feeling that the soul is magnified and that one is invited to make the difficult journey deep within the sacred precincts of being to see the unseeable and know the unknowable. The blues that are so prominent in El Greco's work are invitations to see deeply just as the figures extend our awareness of the human figure as well as the human soul.

I have a reproduction of El Greco's only real landscape, his portrait of the city of Toledo where I can contemplate it every day. I never see through the depths of shadow that enshroud the city to make out the meaning but it always sets my mind to searching for the meaning bound up in the shades of darkness. I think I know but my knowing is still too tentative to venture a revelation of the truth that hides within the mystical meaning. The rich, warm Spanish sunshine must allow room for the clouds that produced the Inquisition and the darker side of the human countenance, and even the noblest expressions of the human spirit have their dark side that is always struggling for its place in the sun. The enigmatic artist who tried to bring the mysticism of eastern orthodoxy abreast with the spirit of St. Francis created the vision of the saints who were seeking to live above the struggle but were ever aware of it even if they had to make a vigorous effort to turn their eyes away from it.

Both color and form became partners as El Greco stretched his imagination to deal with an idea too demanding for the ordinary perception of life. The mystic is always demanding more of the external world in an effort to reveal the spiritual truths that the inner being knows so well. It explains the fact that the mystical vision is never able to find the talent or facility to give expression to the yearning of the spirit so that we are always obliged to be satisfied with approximations. Then we exalt when a master brings the mystical vision within the grasp of our finite minds as El Greco does.

We find the same ability in the creative genius of Marc Chagall. One spring morning we were hiking in the hills of Vermont, Dr. Lawrence

LeShan and myself, talking about the need for a more vigorous explanation of the substance of the mystical perceptions. He burst out with a vigorous expression of his conviction that there must be a clear reflection of the realism of the mystical perception in artistic form. I thought of the skill of Marc Chagall as reflected in the east transept of the cathedral windows in Metz, France. I challenged him to make some time available to go with me to Metz and have a personal encounter with that window which has as its setting the experience of Moses with the burning bush in the wilderness. We agreed then and there to make a private pilgrimage to the cathedral which had been badly damaged by the second World War and had replacements done by modern artists, Marc Chagall being one of them. It was several months before we arrived in Metz.

We parked our rented Peugeot in the parking area next to the cathedral and walked through its portals. We went directly to the east transept and the window depicting Moses and the burning bush. We arranged a chair before the window so that with a minimum of strain the good doctor could have the best view of Chagall's vision. I gave him a pat on the shoulder and a blessing as I said I would be back in an hour. When I came back I interrupted his reverie and he growled, "Leave me alone, it's happening." So I left him alone and they had started to close the cathedral for the evening when I saw him leave the east transept walking as if he were floating with his feet barely touching the floor. He hardly uttered a word all evening and seemed transported by the mystical vision inspired by the work of the artist.

We continued our travels next day and after a few days seeing other cathedrals in northern France and the Rhineland we parted so that he could have a few days hiking in the hills of Greece, a favorite haunt of his. When I returned home I received a call from Eda LeShan, Dr. LeShan's wife, saying that he had left Greece after two days because he was overwhelmed by the effect of Chagall's window in Metz. So in two days he was back sitting in front of that window of Moses and the burning bush. I have talked with him since that experience. He described the

72

powerful effects of the window and the mystical experience that came with it. Physically he said that its effect was so great that he did not have a bite of food or drink during those two days and except for the precaution of drinking water to prevent dehydration he was unaware of the physical aspect of being. His mind traveled far and wide and deep into the realm of perception. He felt filled with healing energy and when he checked on those patients who had been the object of his mystical awareness they reported significant benefits from his intervention. The impact of this mystical experience has been life changing. When he returned to the States he wrote the most significant book of his life, The Medium, The Mystic and the Physicist, and organized a group of his colleagues and students to pursue in depth the implications of his experiences with his mystical awareness.

Quite obviously he has been deeply influenced by his experience and since then has teamed up with Dr. Henry Margenau, the noted physicist in the writing of a discerning book on the understanding of the deeper dimensions of the mystical experience called Van Gogh's Sky and Einstein's Space. Several other books have given depth to the understanding of the nature of the healing power and the nature of the spiritual life. An artist, Chagall, was the creator of a mood that was able to see deeply into the inner being and set something free that soared in different dimensions of the life of the mind and spirit.

Musicians are artists whose approach to a different organ of sensation can be as effective in stimulating a mystical awareness. Music can arouse different sensations but I am thinking primarily of those that help to stimulate the quiet, meditative and exploratory depths of human spirit as found in the music of Bach, Franck and Casals. We could think of many creators of the spiritual or mystical dimension in music for this was characteristic of many Russian composers who come out of a tradition that was steeped in the mystical awareness.

J.S. Bach (1685-1750) developed a musical idiom that was both an art and a language. He gave himself fully to life and religion as it was practiced in his time. One could say that he wrote his heart out and most of what he wrote has been preserved. He set much of the scriptures to music and his oratorios and cantatas are still widely used today. Much of his organ music is unsurpassed and is written with a mathematical precision that shows he was as much at home with the keyboards as he was with his mother tongue. He brought music to a perfection of expression that has not been surpassed and his fugues were brought to their codas and masterly strettos that are a model of musical expression. While he was a specialist in church music with a large component of spiritual awareness he was not unaware of the music of the outside and he brought the secular music of his day to the church so that both the sacred and secular were enriched thereby.

Many are the persons who have been brought to a new level of spiritual realization by a prelude that transformed their mood from that of the secular world to a new perception of the spiritual and mystical world. The essence of worship was the process by which the inner world could be made available for the impact of the message of the spiritual and the music of Bach was eminently designed to invite the spirit to participate at a higher level of perception.

The amazing thing was that the unschooled and the trained were open to the influence of his music. I remember one Sunday morning in Nurenberg when I started early and went to another worship service every hour until noon and four of the several services had a Bach prelude to begin the worship. It was almost taken for granted that there was no better way for inviting the participation of the spirit than the beauty and order of a Bach prelude. What has come to be regarded as appropriate for all worship, Catholic and Protestant, contemporary and traditional, humble and exalted is this music that seems to be so aware of the mystical nature of the human spirit and the universal appeal of Bach in creating the mystical mood. He was not only able to create the mood but he could also perpetuate it for two of his sons followed in his footsteps in making the music that stirs the spirit.

Getting acquainted with those persons who are important to the development of one's mystical nature is more often accidental than planned. The calculating approach doesn't usually work for the mystical impulse is not easily driven into a corner and caught. So it was with my encounter with Cesar Franck, not the most outstanding person in musical history but one who seemed to speak especially to me. It happened that in college I landed a job being the night janitor of the school of music. While it was not an edifying position it did have certain benefits. After the closing hour I had the whole building to myself and could play on the three organs as I willed. Also I had access to the library of recorded music. A professor of music made an appreciative reference to Cesar Franck in class one day about fifty six years ago and that started something that is still going on.

It seems that Franck was one of those souls who had a well-developed mystical nature that seemed to show through every thing he did. Though Franck was a quiet and unassuming person he reflected a special quality in his life. Whether it was in his teaching, his composition and in his playing the church organ in Paris where he spent most of his life, he seemed to touch something in people that made them aware of a deeper nature, a soul within. This was done unobtrusively, almost as if he did not know he was doing it. He did not try to become prominent in his field of special endeavor. While he was alive he did not become famous for his compositions although they were used extensively by other organists.

He wrote oratorios and masses that were used during his lifetime. He wrote only one symphony that was mercilessly criticized by the supposed authorities of his day. He wrote operas that were largely overlooked by the public of his day. But every Sunday he gave the people at the St. Clotilde a quality of worshipful music that was uplifting. His cantata, Ruth, was inspiring and is still performed. He was sincere and earnest and his following in the conservatory and on Sundays had an influence on a new generation of French musicians. He seemed to kindle an awareness of the power of music to reach the depth of the soul. That quality of his has been appreciated with time and now his music is among the more often heard in concert. His D Minor Symphony is one of the most popular today. It is a philosophy of life that enjoys the dancing rhythm as well as the most worshipful. It infuses all of life with its richness of perception and invites those who hear it to enjoy the richer meaning life can provide. For decades Cesar Franck has nourished the mystical dimension of my life.

While his life was lived entirely within the nineteenth century his mystical sensitivity makes it possible in his music whether for piano, organ, chorus or orchestra, to speak with a universal appeal to all those who are aware of the depth of their own being. He has nourished the mystical awareness of several generations of those whose souls are readily available to the sounds of music.

I have always been sensitive to human needs and so have always been concerned about those who fought against tyranny and the efforts to repress the human spirit. So I became deeply interested in the struggle of the Spanish people against fascism and the brutal Franco regime. I became chairman of the unit of the Committee to Aid Spanish Democracy of which Bishop Francis J. McConnell was national chairman. I began to hear of an idealistic cellist named Pablo Casals who was giving great aid to the movement. Finally the combined power of Mussolini and Hitler aided by the blockade of our own government was able to defeat the forces of freedom, but I had learned of a little man with a great heart who stood firm for the rights of man. I never met the man and never was closer than the stage and the balcony but that man has been one of the great men of mystical awareness whose life has been an inspiration to me.

Early in his life he was able to develop a rare music talent and he dedicated it to an instrument that was not considered a prime possibility for the virtuoso performer. Undeterred by the generally low opinion of his chosen instrument, the cello, he set out to try to develop its possibilities. He found new mellowness, undetected possibilities, and great potential in the cello and dedicated it and his art to the welfare of humanity. When he gave a concert in Puerto Rico the audiences winged their way south to hear the greatest master of the cello who had ever lived. He lived long enough to see the final triumph of democracy in his beloved Spain, but he had made a stand for the human spirit against the forces of fascism that will go down in history as an example of the best of music and mystical understanding. In the midst of those who would destroy human freedom and reduce the wonder of human life and its possibilities it is challenging to find those whose art and spirit refuse to bend their lives to a lesser perception of the human sacredness that is glimpsed in the commitments of the mystic. Casals refused to compromise his values no matter what forces were aligned against him. He showed that human values and artistic excellence could be nourished by an uncompromising human spirit.

The artists of the world have always chosen to exalt a way of knowing that was not bound up with the crasser measurements of human dignity. Many are the scientists who feel the limitations of the scientific method and in their deep inner beings turn to poetry and painting to express the self that is stifled by the stark measurements of mathematics and the slide rule or the supercomputer. They add humanity to their scientific searches and in the end add a dimension to the understanding of the human spirit. We have looked at a few persons who have given richness to the human quest through both their art and their mystical spirit. They not only show that it can be done but they challenge us to join them in doing it. In a world that too often seems to be racing toward self destruction there desperately needs to be a clear definition of another way, the way of the artist who is also a mystic.

Chapter 8

THE MYSTICAL ELEMENT IN PREACHING

When you spend more than fifty years in doing something there is a strong possibility that you have developed some ideas about what you are doing. And yet the activity of preaching is largely bound up in unexamined efforts that are made up usually of desperation, plagiarism and a flavoring of inspiration. I suppose it would be no exaggeration to say that preaching involves more time in speaking and listening than any other form of communication. Hundreds of thousands of speakers then spend billions of words every year in a process that has been going on for centuries. Such a mass effort may be largely unexamined but it cannot be easily assumed to be meaningless. It has survived in varied cultures in differing times and it invites examination as a significant human venture.

Could it be that the longterm human effort is explained by a mystical impulse that finds a meaning in an impulse rather than in a logical process?

I well remember that Sunday in 1933 when I first mounted a pulpit I could call my own. I looked down at a group of about fifty people who were quite obviously filled with misgivings. During the next few years I was scheduled to confront them with about a hundred specially prepared messages to sustain their souls. I was prepared with four seminary-enriched samples. It is to my credit that two of those gems were never used. During the next week I found out that my predecessor had skillfully fleeced many members of the church with borrowings that were sworn to secrecy. Soon their common plight was known and my heritage was doubt and distrust. But also I was quickly thrown into the maelstrom of human misery and suffering. My first sermon that week was delivered at a funeral and I had the sense to know that nothing I had brought with me from seminary was pertinent to my setting.

In 1933 the country was enduring the depths of the Great Depression. Added to the national crisis was the local depression that came from the perfidy of a shepherd who had betrayed his flock. I soon realized that my first task was to serve these people so well that they would replace their image of their last pastor with trust and confidence that was unshakeable. I said nothing about my predecessor but went to work to do everything possible to do and be what these people wanted and needed. I was born five miles away from my parish, for Centerport was three miles East of Huntington and my birthplace was two miles west of that north shore town. These places had lots of intermarriage and close relationships. Before the first week was over, I found that I was related, though not closely, to several families. Before a month had gone by, I was aware of a kinship to more than half of the membership of my flock. They soon realized that I had been put, through no fault of my own, into a difficult position and their basic sense of fair play led them to my support.

Also another advantageous circumstance was that my status in life invited consideration. I was a young bachelor. I quickly noticed a beautiful young woman who taught church school effectively and sang solos in the choir. She was of a prominent family of the parish. She was of gracious personality and a fine character and I felt that she was the kind of person I would like to share my life with. I had very little to share at that stage of the game but my persistence finally won out and ere long we were man and wife. That it was a fortunate choice has been attested by fifty-four years of partnership and devotion and it is not over yet. That first parish with all of the problems that I inherited was a blessing for it gave me a most wonderful partner for the trying life that the parish ministry was to bring. I soon realized that the pastor's task was threefold, preaching, pastoral care and parish supervision, they were like a three legged milking stool, for they were equally important and a failure of one gave unbalanced performance. It was the best possible place to study the pastoral function. I soon learned to take what was taught in seminary with modification. I learned to listen to my people to see what they thought and needed. I asked one day what on old sea captain thought made a good sermon and he quoted the scripture "Feed my sheep". I always remembered his words. As time went along my experience accumulated and I began to arrive at ideas I wanted to share. I started writing articles for professional and church papers sharing those ideas. I developed more respect for the written word as 1 began to get feedback from readers. With time I received invitations to write books along the lines of some of my articles. Then I started to get invitations from seminaries to speak for them, and finally to get opportunities to accept faculty assignments. In time one of my books was chosen to be included in a special printing of the so-called ten most important books on preaching in the last century. They did listen to a preacher in a local parish.

When I was transferred to a manufacturing town in Connecticut, I was faced with another type of congregation. These were people with a short attention span. They were used to working with machinery that was demanding and if you did not pay attention you could loose a finger. Quite different from the listeners in my last parish, who spent lots of time as harvesters of the bays and sounds on their own terms. The persons who were geared to a machine were obliged to become attentive to the machine. When they attended church they settled back to rest during the sermon for they were not attuned to long listening. So I developed the homiletic plan of using lots of short illustrations with a brief application. Also I began the practice of asking people after church what the sermon was about. At first there was no response and they even acted as if the question were impertinent. Why should anyone ask about their private resting time?

Then I developed a time for discussion and feedback. Coffee was served and they knew that they were a part of a conversation where the preacher talked to them about something where their opinion was explored and they were in turn expected to respond. After a time we developed quite a lively and spirited talk back session. People would respond if they were sure that they were really being talked to. I asked one new member of the congregation what the preaching was like in the church of her previous membership and she responded that the preacher was always scratching them where they did not itch. An awful lot of this effort of preachers was, I felt, a wasted effort. So I wrote a book that was a simple effort to give a direction to this practice that occupied so much of people's time during Sunday mornings. "How to Preach to People's Needs" was the name of the book. Many young preachers used it as a text and the sermons that were included as illustrations were preached from coast to coast during subsequent years as the book was reprinted again and again as a textbook.

I read the letters that came pouring in from many of my colleagues who were burdened by the task of presenting each Sunday some utterance of significance. Often the wells were pumped dry and then there was nothing to do but use old notebooks or engage in the demeaning practice of copying what others had done. So I decided to write another book and address it to the problem of preaching that was seldom mentioned, "A Psychology for preaching." This was immediately made a selection of the pulpit book club and really started a careful study of what happened as the result of a sermon. It was built around an experiment I had done comparing the reaction of a congregation following two quite different kinds of sermons. One was the repressive-inspirational type of sermon,—the type that was always preached by Norman Vincent Peale with lovely and inspiring poems and heroic stories but not much focus on the truth of life and not much help for those struggling with cruel fate. On alternate weeks I preached a sermon that focused on the reality of human experience and ended with a question that forced the listener to examine responsibility and take action to change circumstance. The experiment with the two sermon types continued for twenty weeks with careful evaluation of responses by the congregation by skilled and trained observers. The responses were quite interesting. One obsessive compulsive neurotic told an observer after the series had progressed a while that it was funny but the preacher seemed to preach a good sermon every other week. After a repressive-inspirational sermon people stood around outside the door on the lawn and laughed and talked joyfully. After the analytic sermons they were disinclined to do this but went toward their cars as if they didn't want to talk. But other forms of behavior were noticed which were considered significant for after the repressive-inspirational sermons practically no pastoral counseling was instituted. On the other hand, in the ten weeks following the analytical sermons, more than two hundred and forty counseling sessions were instituted.

It was quite obvious that there was a sharp difference in the behavior of the congregation depending on the nature of the sermon. This rather simple experiment became the basis for a number of graduate degree studies of the effects of preaching. In seminaries the emphasis seems to have turned away from topical preaching and biblical exposition to life exploration and shared experience. I developed an approach to sermon preparation that seemed to me to guarantee several ideas that I thought important. Instead of spending the first part of the week working on the sermon for the next Sunday, I turned the process around. During my summer vacation I outlined the preaching schedule for the year and outlined the sermon in a preliminary type of overview of the topic so that it could be filled in at any time in the year. Then each week I would spend as much time with my people as possible thinking about the subject of the sermon and getting as much input as possible. Sometimes I would do this quite directly and at other times it would be general listening and talking about life situations. My reading and my thinking would be aimed at the subject of next Sunday with all the thinking shared as much as possible. There would be a year's worth of accumulated thinking and some emerging ideas as we got close to the appointed Sunday. I would review the notes and outlines before I retired Saturday night but would not consider anything final until I slept on it Saturday night. Then I would get up about four o'clock Sunday morning when my mind was clear and I was refreshed and would look at my congregation in terms of its thoughts and needs as I had heard them expressed in the days leading up to this morning. My mind worked clearly and well in the early morning hours and I was ready for the privileged hour when it came.

Using this method of preparation I combined the long and careful incubation of ideas with the open mind that was sensitive to the last thought that might occur. I always had a pretty good idea of what was going but my mind was never congealed in advance of my encounter with the congregation. I have often been asked what would I do if I overslept but it never happened. Also I was asked what happened if no inspiration came but I guarded against that by making my people part of the preparation process. They had always been there in advance to ask the important questions and I could always refer to them. I prepared a full outline before each sermon and then left it on my desk so that nothing would stand between me and my first duty, which was to pay attention to the congregation. I usually preached twice on Sunday mornings and although the sermons were supposed to be the same, when I compared the tapes it was amazing to see how different they had become in the actual delivery. It was the active encounter with a congregation that made the difference.

Although the potential congregation was very much involved in both the preparation and the delivery, I made sure that there was never a chance that anyone could identify anything personal. Even with the use of personal references they were modified so that even the person involved could in no way identify the subject of the illustration. This could usually be done by a change of a pronoun, a date or a place. It is important to use narrative material in a sermon but the person referred to in the narrative should always be protected unless it is a public figure and the matter referred to is a matter of public knowledge. Even then one can never be too careful about matters of privacy between a pastor and the people. There are other related subjects where the type of material focused on the "psychology of preaching". It was the first time some of these subjects were treated in book form and it was published here and abroad in several editions. It had quite an influence in bringing some of the unexamined aspects of this familiar form of communication into closer scrutiny.

Still there were some things about preaching that I had never examined closely. What was there about this form of largely unexamined communication that guaranteed its longevity? It was here that I began to look for the mystical unknown quality where deep seems to speak to deep and where a beyond merely rational quality appears to take over. Some preachers say that there are times when another entity seems to take over and they feel empowered by a force not easily explained. There are elements of tradition and the influence of the arts that contribute to this feeling. I have friends who are college professors who admit that preaching a sermon for half an hour takes more out of them than teaching for several hours. What seems to make the difference? Being lifted up and placed behind a pulpit seems to put a special burden on a mortal who for a time seems to be trying to speak for God. Is it that the preacher does not really feel competent to take on this exalted role? They are forced to assume that for which they feel burdened and inadequate. I have asked the question many times and have yet to receive an adequate answer. So I decided to give myself to the deeper meaning of preaching. What is the deeper meaning of this type of communication? How can we define and detail then this deeper meaning and explain its origin? It was about this time that I received an invitation from Boston School of Theology to give some of their lectures on preaching. This I was glad to do for it would give me a chance to refine some of my thinking on communications depth dimension.

The Boston University Annual Lectures on Preaching is probably the most prestigious lectureship in this area of study. Its history has had some of the best-known and more illustrious practitioners of this special form of communicating. I was asked to share the podium with Dr. Robert McCracken, of Riverside Church in New York. He spoke after dinner and I had the block of time the next morning. I focused on the changes that took place in the minds and spirits of the listeners that reflected their deeper perceptions. I think the lectures caused quite a stir because for the first time it was assumed that the subject could be approached scientifically and that the assumptions could be looked at as encompassing more than talking and listening. It took into consideration the mood and manner of homiletics plus a consideration of the mystical nature of the encounter of preacher and listener. This meant that much of what is characterized as and passed for preaching must be discounted as irrelevant for there is no serious meeting of mind and spirit.

In serious and inspired preaching the preacher enters into an engagement with the listeners to wrestle with a proposition and assess the movement that is achieved in the active encounter. Unless something happens they might as well have been watching a football game. I was asked to present my concepts many times in the years that followed and I hope I made some impression on my colleagues of the cloth. After the time in Marsh Chapel, on the campus of Boston University I was asked to become a member of the faculty of the school as professor of preaching. When we reviewed the terms of the relationship, although they were most gracious and generous, I decided against the offer because it would be too confining. About the last of the trilogy on preaching-it is still in the works and I hope even yet to complete the writing of the book on communication's depth dimension.

I have had the chance in the quietness and leisure of retirement to think over the admonitions of those who were my professors through the years. I have departed from their ways as time evolved but each of them in their way taught me many valuable things and left me with many valuable insights. My friend and counselor Halford E. Luccock was a master in relevant speech and I owe him much for the insight into language as a tool. Harry Emerson Fosdick was the model for the active engagement of the mind of the listener and I had the honor of writing his biography in the History of Christian Thought. Hugh Black was a dour Scotsman who gave me insight into expository sermons though I gave little heed to his teaching. John Schroeder was an expert in the practice of social preaching. Lynn Harold Hough specialized in relating sermons to broad cultural movements in literature and the arts. George Buttrick was of special interest to me because he had the skill that kindled a response in others. I followed him some years after he left one parish. He was remembered as thoughtful and, after he got warmed up, quite dynamic and always well liked for his sincerity of purpose. All of my teachers offered me something of value but I had the feeling that one had to develop one's own style in order to be true to one's own being.

I think that the main contribution to any special understanding of the preaching function was gained from my special interest in psychology. I was always wondering what was going on in the mind and emotions of the people with whom I shared the hour of worship and especially the time of the sermon. I was specifically concerned about their attitude of mind and emotion as they approached the sermon. I used many methods to accomplish that end. I would ask them before the service if they were preaching on the subject what they would say. Often I would pursue the subject so that we would get deeper into the matter. If I would quote them it would be anonymously. I was interested in getting their thoughts and not of exposing any differences that might be observed. The why and how of their ways of thinking helped to sharpen up ways of thinking as the premise for ways of acting. I was concerned about making them aware of the fact that the way they thought and acted did make a difference and that their religious thinking was an important part of their total acting out, their way of living. It was somewhat like Fosdick's way of engaging a congregation in a major issue of life but I tried to make it more personal and related to the particular lives of the congregation. It was an effort to try to help people to better understand themselves.

As I look back on fifty-some years of this special form of communication, I am still intrigued by what happens. The same sermon that may put some persons to sleep may institute life changes in others that are major forces for modification. Something beyond reason seems to be operating to add meaning to the basic language. Some of the more influential preachers have voice characteristics and mannerisms that detract from the pleasure of listening but this does not seem to matter when deep speaks to deep. It seems that a direct line to the core of being with life changing results is possible without following all the rules of rhetoric. Having spent half a century trying to look deeply at this form of communication, I must admit that some things about it still baffle me. Perhaps the mystical meaning of the Holy Spirit has to account for those things that are beyond our understanding.

The third book in my trilogy on preaching is outlined and I have about ninety thousand words written, but I sometimes wonder if it will ever be finished. It has to be reduced in size and increased in wisdom. There are times when I have grave doubts about my ability to accomplish the task. Some things become more mysterious the more closely they are examined. Michael Polanyi writes of Tacit Dimension, that something else that seems to be beyond easy analysis and comprehension. Noam Chomsky looks to a mystical dimension in communication that gives the unexplainable factor to language wherein is found its most remarkable quality. It may well be that in this mystical quality of human speech takes on its most important function. The quality of this something added to life and understanding is approached more effectively through preaching at its best and poetry at its best and there are times when the two art forms seem to share that other dimension. Maybe preaching in its own peculiar way comes closer to being the language of the true mystic.

Chapter 9

THE MYSTIC AS STREET FIGHTER

One likes to think of the pastoral life as calm and peaceful but that is not always the case. It is not that choice is always left in our own hands but that the antagonistic forces tend to make the choices and we have to take action as the situation may dictate. Sometimes the devil and the forces of evil are aggressive and there is nothing to do but to meet them head on.

I had not been in Connecticut long before I had a chance to know some of the aggression at first hand. With the aid of some of my fellow clergymen we decided to do some education and fund raising for the Spanish democratic movement under the auspices of the North American Committee to Aid Spanish Democracy. My Bishop, Francis J. McConnell, was the Chairman. We decided that we would show a film entitled Spain in Flames. We were immediately denied a permit by the chief of police in Waterbury. We figured it was the right of any group to carry on an educational and fund raising program even though the Catholic Church might be opposed. So we contacted the American Civil Liberties Union to see if they thought we had a case. They said that we unquestionably did and that they would take charge. So a case was heard before the superior court of the State—Jackson vs. Roach. There was much publicity and newspaper headlines called attention to the upcoming court process. The local and state government was generally considered to be corrupt and yet no one had been willing to challenge the corrupt political machine because they were well entrenched and seemed to have lots of power. Everyone knew of the skullduggery but no one seemed willing to challenge the forces of evil.

I was surprised by the large amount of support that came our way. A clergyman seemed to be the ideal community figure to face the corruption. The weeks leading up to the court appearance were filled with all sorts of actions designed to embarrass the ones who challenged the authority of the entrenched regime. When the day of the hearing came I was apprehensive for the ACLU lawyer and I were arrayed against a battery of lawyers from the city and state. But the upshot of the matter was that the court issued a dictum in behalf of those who wanted the protection of the police rather than the censorship of a police department that wanted to take the law into its own hands.

The case was heard shortly before elections and the finding of the court gave some support to the people who opposed the corrupt regime, enough to turn some of the rascals out of office and the new officers of the city and state led to a clean sweep with 23 politicians of the city and state going to jail or being heavily fined. My District Superintendent wrote a letter that said in part, "the evil man fleeth when no man persueth but he goes a lot faster if someone is after him". I learned that nothing seems to produce corrective action like guilt that stirs the mind of the evil one. In spite of the outcome of the court hearing and its aftermath some of my own church people said that they did not think it was the role of their pastor to take people to court.

I learned that when you are right and have the truth on your side it provides a way of doing things that seems to be effective and had better be used than not. But it is important to be prepared for the methods used by the unscrupulous for they are not careful about their methods or the consequences. After the publicity that was attendant upon the court proceedings I had a chance to be better known in the community. I was asked to speak to many and varied groups.

One day a woman called and asked if I would speak to her group, which she identified as the Lithuanian American Literary Society. I asked what was the religious inclination of the group and she indicated that they were all atheists. I, of course, accepted, for who would not accept such a challenge. In the working class section of town over a saloon I found the location of the literary society. Most of the people present talked with a foreign accent and I sensed a hostile atmosphere in the crowd.

After a general conversation within the group the woman who had called me before and greeted me at the door rose to quiet the group. The big mustached group quieted and seemed to glower as they were prepared to listen. I talked of Moses who was the first labor leader in history and the trials he had in getting his people organized. I talked of the powerful opposition and the unusual methods that had to be used under the circumstances. They began to show interest. I told of the adventures of some of the Old Testament prophets who led movements against the rich and powerful. Then I shifted to more modern times with John Wesley talking at the entrance to the mine shafts in England and the organization of workers at the shop gates to hear a message of their worth in the plan of God. I ended by referring to the social creed of the churches and I asked if they had any questions.

That was the beginning of an interesting hour of encounter and of years of active interest in an educational program among people who wanted to learn but had had little chance. These people in their labored language asked questions for an hour and prefaced most questions with the phrase "in the old country they told us, but you say". We had a spirited and no-holds-barred question and answer period and I could tell there was conflict brewing in the hall. Finally the woman in charge called an end to the questions and then there was a long and heated argument, which I could tell, was directed toward me although I couldn't understand a word of what was said. Finally the woman in charge quieted the crowd and said "Mr. Minister Jackson, we would like to invite you to our next meeting to say more on these things."

This led to a series of shop gate meetings and eventually I was teaching in the New Haven Labor College on a regular basis. I was a volunteer member of the National Religion and Labor Foundation teaching courses in American History, Parliamentary Law and Social Change. This was an interesting and productive period of my life and ministry and was a chance to grow in understanding of the hopes and aspirations of the more recent flood of immigrants who came to these shores. Soon I had a chance to identify more closely with the labor movement when we were called upon to work with those who were providing the materials of war for our friends abroad who were carrying the burdens of the battle.

When it came time for me to register for the draft I was faced with a moral dilemma. As a clergyman I was entitled to exemption from the demands of the draft. But as a citizen I could not ask others to bear the burdens and run the risks of my citizenship. So I rejected my exemption and when my number and status was due I was classified 1A and reported for duty. I realized that I was causing a problem for the classifications officer for they had no place to put me. First they tried to put me in a psychiatric class but after a psychiatric exam they found me disgustingly normal and so asked me to return to my draft board and be reclassified to meet the requirements of their regulations. I was in the army in no time flat, and after attending chaplain's school, was then selected for the air force. Only three out of the class of two hundred were so selected. From the time when my history of labor organizing activity was discovered, I was assigned a military intelligence officer as a roommate. After a while they admitted to me the nature of their assignment and some of them with time became life long friends. Such is the nature of the caution that guards our national security. My first assignment was as Chaplain in a replacement center in New Mexico where I had supervisory role over the nuclear base at Alamogordo. I remained there until after the explosion of the first A-bomb. Then I had assignments in Europe and Africa before being released from Active service at the Pentagon in June 1946.

I was then assigned to the parish from which my father was retiring in the industrial section of Bridgeport, where I soon picked up the activities that occupied me before the war. A reformed government in New York had driven the Mafia out of the city and into New Jersey and Connecticut. Bridgeport had been a likely center for their activities and they soon controlled the financial activities of the local unions with the shop stewards controlling the numbers games in the factories. At that time I was elected president of the Pastor's Association, an influential group of about a hundred members. Wives of workers brought complaints to me of the mob's control of the numbers games so that the take home pay of workers was drastically reduced and the families were suffering severely.

Our association took action to have the district attorney enforce the laws and drive the mafia out of town. We soon found that the mafia was not so easily driven from town and they put up a vigorous fight. The home of the state's attorney was burned and there was no easy end of the actions against me, my family and other members of the association. Threats of evisceration, emasculation and other similar treatments were promised if the campaign against them was not called off. We became yet more determined for many of the clergy had never before been directly challenged by the organized forces of evil. The forces of law were galvanized into steady action once they knew that the community was behind them. After a few court trials and action against them the mafia quietly withdrew from the city and remained quiescent for a few years before they made their presence felt again. It was another illustration of the value of the righteous forces of a city making a stand and holding their position. It was strenuous and not always pleasant but it verified that the evil ones "fleeth" and go faster if they know they are being chased.

Some of the more reactionary members of my parish were always on the alert for an occasion to find fault with my ministry. If I stepped out of line on what they considered pastoral decorum they were quick to let me know. Just such an occasion came about with the nomination of Henry Wallace for president as an independent. I was asked if I would appear on the preliminary session to give the church's position on war and peace. As a recently returned veteran I was glad to support the church's position and urge others to accept its strong statement. When it came time for the state convention to be called to order I was there ready to give the official position of my church on war and peace. I was introduced and after a brief comment read the New York Conference statement on the subject and then returned to my parish to prepare for the morrow, which was Sunday.

I was at church early and did not take time to read the morning paper. The pastoral relations committee met at 9 a.m. to consider appropriate action and faced me with the headlines and a chance to resign before the morning service. This gave me an opportunity to explain my action before the committee made its statement and they were chagrined to know that they had their story inaccurately and so nothing came of their effort to put me on the spot. In fact the chairman of the pastoral relations committee who had taken the lead in the action against me actually moved that I be unanimously invited to return as pastor at the next annual meeting.

In 1952 I was called to the pastorate of what I considered one of the strongest churches in the conference. A largely professional congregation with strong leadership capabilities lived in this high-class suburb and worked in New York City. They also possessed liberal traits.

I was soon elected to head a psychiatric clinic with special interest in children and their parents. I carried on this activity in addition to my regular parish load. The clinic's liberal stance quickly brought us into conflict with conservative forces in the four communities served by the clinic. They decided to attack us at the point of our finances. They tried to get the Community Chest in the four towns to terminate their support because Dr. Goodwin Watson had flirted briefly with socialism and was active in liberal politics. We were, in effect, tried by the community through guilt by association. The American Legion led the opposition. The Westchester Legion was well organized and had financial support. The Guidance Center and the American Legion carried on an active campaign through the newspapers, which seemed to thrive on such conflicts. By carrying on our program with dignity and integrity of purpose we were able to win the support of liberal elements of the community and finally won on all fronts. The Guidance Center more than doubled its community support during this encounter and remains as one of the strongest social agencies in the region. We did not have to retreat on any front and grew because of the favorable publicity.

But some groups did not enjoy taking a public licking, so if they could not win by one method they sought alternatives. This was during the time of Senator Joseph McCarthy. It was difficult to build up opposition to McCarthy because of the fear he was able to generate. I was asked to write a public letter to be signed by the clergy of the county. The letter was to build on the Bill of Rights and emphasize that if we did not use it we might lose it. After a month I was still the only one who was willing to publicly support the Bill of Rights and the declaration of support for the constitutional privileges. Those were times when fear was strong in the country but those who took advantage of the climate were cowardly souls who didn't understand the strength of those who believed strongly and were willing to run risks and accept consequences.

The letter was finally published with only one signature. As a result our congressman nominated me to serve as honorary chaplain of the House of Representatives. This I did with pleasure and have lived to see that era in our history eclipsed by more of sanity and goodwill.

But lest you think that was the end of the matter a group of conservative members of my own church took it upon themselves to purge the church of my nefarious influence. They called themselves the Circuit Riders grasping on the honored tradition of the past and the heroism of those who fought against the wilds and loneliness of the deprivations of the frontiers to advance their faith and their church. Instead they tried to attack those who made courageous stands for principle. They used much the same method as the KKK who anonymously crept up in the night to try to scare people who were defenseless. I was making about 250 lectures a year and it was not surprising to find that the circuit riders had been there first leaving a piece of literature on each chair. It was made up mostly of quotes taken out of context and always using the same material. I was usually asked if I wanted them picked up and destroyed and I always responded that I had nothing to hide and that I would enjoy exploring the message of such groups and their manner of delivering it. They attack people behind their backs with the implication that they are vulnerable and covering something up which they are making bold to expose. With proper explanation and context there is nothing left of their attack and the tables are turned against them. I found that any such attack could be used to good advantage if handled properly. Any effort at explanation that grew from an assumption of weakness would not work, but an attack that was based on facts with no apology usually seemed effective. I surmise that I faced more than my share of such assaults and as far as I know they were all turned around to serve a good purpose by bold confrontation and no attempt to make excuses.

My father was a big help in learning how to handle that type of person. He grew up in a family that tried to do a positive work in those turbulent days of reconstruction following the Civil War. My grandfather had started a school in Tennessee for Black children and the KKK took a dim view of Northerners who were interfering with the social patterns of the South. After repeated efforts at assassination my grandfather got the leading citizens of the region together and boldly faced the issue. As a Mason and a Christian pastor he had much in common with them, and hoped they would act on that rather than some antagonism that grew from racial conflicts that had already been put behind them. The confrontation put their misunderstanding behind them. My father used the same method for resolving conflicts. Never back down but always be conciliatory.

My feeling was that wherever possible it was desirable to work out problems with a courageous facing of issues. Where that was not possible it was always best to face the problem in public with complete candor and as much personal involvement as the situation would allow. Nothing gave an adversary an advantage like the show of weakness or timidity. Similarly nothing was as disarming as a completely open and honest facing of basic issues. In the kind of issues as those mentioned in this chapter it was often not possible to meet the adversaries openly but only meet them in stray phone calls in the wee small hours of the morning and then only in veiled threats and degrading language. But here too it was important never to stoop to the level of the attacker but always to use the language and the methods of the one who would be fair if given that chance to deal with the issue honorably.

Some of the activities involving the Mafia cannot be managed in quietness and goodwill. Their cowardly way of proceeding cannot be met with dignity. Those nights of repeated calls to our home, answered by my wife, Estelle, left their mark but Estelle was never made to lose her calmness and after a time they gave up their nefarious efforts. Death threats were never pleasant but as long as they remained only threats their perpetrators could be treated as cowards and that helped to keep things in perspective.

The quiet life of retirement is the best vantage point for looking back on such events. While I am still in favor of justice and goodwill there is now little chance to be involved in crusades. Perhaps we tend to be more conservative as old age moves in upon us. Or perhaps we just become tired. Now in this peaceful setting we don't have as much to bother us—just the fundamentalists who have such a narrow perspective that they see little. Now they seem to be the only ones who object to me. Makes me feel useless indeed. I am glad that through the years I have stood for more important issues. I hope that my stands have done some good. It has been an interesting struggle and I have enjoyed the intensity and challenge of it all.

Chapter 10

MYSTICISM AND THE MANAGEMENT OF CRISIS

Very often in life, important things that happen are the result of circum-locution, that is, you back into them inadvertently. That was the way it was with me and crisis psychology. I didn't set out to develop such a discipline. Several things came together to make it possible. I had, for quite a time, felt dissatisfaction with the intellectual basis for much that went under the label of pastoral care. As I was giving a series of lectures under the auspices of the National Council on Mental Health at a semi-nary in the middle west, the professor who introduced me with a sly bit of humor said, "There have been three men who have influenced my thinking deeply; one was Anton Boisen who was the pioneer in religion and mental health, another was Russell Dicks who was the pioneer in religion and health, and the third one is the pioneer in thinking about religion and life crises such as death and grief, and he is alive where the other two have gone to reap their cosmic reward and it is my pleasure to present him to you now in the flesh, Edgar Jackson." I realized that I was being put in rather select company but I became aware of something else that I hadn't been cognizant of before and that was that there was a more general recognition of my leadership in crisis psychology.

If I was recognized as the leader in the new field I should do something to confirm that place. If there was a new psychological discipline emerging I should write the textbook that would give substance and direction to the emerging thought on the subject. At about that time I discovered the writings of a physician who also had degrees in psychology, psychiatry and theology that gave her an amazing grasp of the relevant disciplines. Flanders Dunbar had an active interest in pastoral care and had also written the definitive book in psychosomatic medicine, <u>The Emotions And Bodily Change</u>. I accepted this as the raw material for establishing the relationship between pastoral care and bodily behavior, or as it is more commonly referred to, illness and disease. I made this book my second bible and as I did my hospital work I would check the medical chart and then check the Dunbar book. I soon developed a working relationship between the two that could give my pastoral work a more specific direction.

I began to develop quite a bit of confidence in the approach to patients and confirmed my confidence by frequent conversations with my physician friends. This grew into ten years of teaching in a medical school and brought closer together the work of the pastor as a crisis psychologist and the physician as a practitioner of the medical side of the specialization. I felt that my experience was adequate to warrant writing a textbook in crisis psychology for as yet there had been no general textbook covering this area of specialization. The chronology of my developing interest was not precise but generally speaking the relation of my developing interest bore on one another and helped to produce the incentive that bore fruit in a book.

The book was finally published in 1974 as <u>Coping With The Crises In Your Life</u>. This was the title settled on by the publisher and I guess it has not done the book any harm for it has been selected three times as a professional book club choice. It was designed as an introduction to the discipline for college students so it tried to establish boundaries and relate to the other personality sciences. It has served its purpose well and for those who want to get acquainted with the subject matter of related fields it is a rather painless way of doing so.

During these years of development and writing I was also engaged in a program of rather extensive lecturing to university, seminary and professional groups. I averaged between 250 and 300 lectures a year and more than anything else that I know of helped spread the word concerning crisis psychology and crisis management and identified me with the developing discipline. There were some schools where I was expected to reappear year after year to keep them abreast of developments in my specialization. In this way I was able to keep the pressure on for a subtle revolution in the way pastoral care was considered.

It was easy to promote this kind of a gentle revolution in the basic assumptions regarding pastoral care for it was not difficult to point out the idea that people move toward the pastoral person when they are confronted with crises in their personal lives. This seems to be increasingly so now that a growing percent of those who are assuming pastoral responsibility are women with their greater sensitivity. Society and the church have too long been misled by some of the misconceptions of Freud. Our day is correcting some of these errors and bringing new warmth and understanding into the care with which human problems are considered and acted upon.

For the first time in history pastoral care has the feeling that it is proceeding on a valid scientific and experimental basis. One of the efforts of this development has been that several hospitals have developed wellness clinics and pain clinics. These have proved to be valid and useful as we better understand and manage the ways in which organic behavior is related to emotional and volitionally controlled behavior. As it is demonstrated in the clinical setting it is accepted as valid where no amount of lecturing has been able to alter the resistance to these ideas by some practitioners.

In a class at the wellness clinic a Major seemed to be in discomfort so I asked him what seemed to be the matter. He replied that he had a splitting headache. I walked from the podium to his chair and stood behind it and placed my hands gently on his forehead and the neck over the atlas vertebra and held them there for a few moments long enough to completely recenter his consciousness. Then after a brief time I asked how he was doing. In a baffled manner he asked where the headache had gone and added that he had better go out on the ward. He rose and left the room shaking his head and after he had gone down the hall a hundred feet or so he stuck his head in the door again and said that he would still like to know where that headache had gone. Nothing seems to work to convince us of the wonders of the power of the mind over the body like experiencing it at work in our own being.

In the hospital they have made it a practice to order the patients to spend three days in the wellness clinic after they have completed their medical treatment focusing their attention on how to stay well. They consider what made them sick and how they control their behavior. They not only consider the idea behind their wellness but they practice how they can reinforce the ideas that are beneficial. They have established through medical records that this is an effective method of cutting down on the return trips to the hospital. It is not only a way of reducing expense but it is a way of producing better health among their clientele. Nothing produces conviction as fast as the experience of the patient although those who witness it are not far behind.

This recasting of the concept of pastoral care is far reaching. For instance the pastoral person has traditionally thought of communication

102

as a process that is primarily centered on telling someone or a group of someones what they need to know in order to achieve a good life. This gives authority to preaching and this authority seeps over into every other aspect of pastoral communication. To take that authority away from a pastor leaves a weakened concept of the pastoral role. The concept of communication reflected in the writing and teaching of Jurgen Ruesch is so new that it has not had a chance to acquire an authority of its own, but it holds great promise of an even greater authority when it has established itself in the minds of those who understand its promise.

Jurgen Ruesch is an Austrian who came to this country early in the time of Hitler. He has taught and written in this country for four decades and has become a leading interpreter of the therapeutic use of language. I found his four books on communication basic to my understanding of the new concept of language as the core of pastoral understanding in its use. The first was <u>Communication; The Matrix Of Psychiatry,</u> which spoke of how language receives what is going on in the core of being and is essential to listening wisely. The second book, <u>Disturbed Communication,</u> shows how pathological conditions are revealed in common speech and is essential to listening with the evaluative ear. The third book, <u>Therapeutic Communication,</u> shows how speech could be used as corrective. The fourth book, <u>Nonverbal Communication,</u> was made up largely of pictures that illustrated the theme of the text. Taken together these books give the best interpretation of language as it reveals the inner person. The books have been around for some time but I don't think they have been surpassed in value for the understanding they give of language as a key to the inner being.

There has been a tendency among clergy to over value their own words and to consider as relatively unimportant the words of those who speak to them. At times there has seemed to be an impatience with the language of others. It was almost as if we were being tolerant of others until they finished their useless prattle and were ready to listen again to our worthy words. After reading Ruesch, pastors would have quite a different concept of the spoken word, both their own and others. They would realize that there might be much more value in listening than they had assumed. The role of the pastoral person would have to be reevaluated appreciably.

I have traveled this country from corner to corner and have always proclaimed the values of the Rueschian doctrine concerning language and I hope some of the seed has fallen on fertile ground. While I am anxious for the pastoral ministry to use all of the insight of the other personality sciences, I would not have it sell itself short for the traditions of pastoral care bring to the therapeutic relationship treasures that are unmatched in any other discipline when properly understood and applied.

One of the difficulties of ministering to persons in crisis is that very often they talk in opposites. For some reason people in crisis try to protect their real feelings from even those who are close to them. Sometimes they can be overcome by insistence. In response to a simple question there may be an evasive answer. This may be met by a comment such as "No, I mean how do you really feel deep inside?" If they are protecting against what they fear is insincerity they may start again and really open up to their inner being. Or it may be that their protectiveness goes deeper and a more patient approach will have to be employed.

Some of the thought patterns that have to do with crises as they are effected by language have been illuminated by philosophical approaches to language in recent decades. The whole effect of Freudian thought has given to language a new and deeper meaning. The effect of the unconscious on speech gives insight into human behavior not understood before. Then too the whole emphasis of the existential movement gave a more meaningful interpretation to language both spoken and written. When we add to that the powerful influence that the emphasis of science and logical positivism has on the academic community you can see how the old fashioned approach to common speech has been modified in recent years.

But these things have not been happening in a vacuum. Noam Chomsky has become perhaps the most powerful influence in language and its theory in contemporary thought. His thinking is more conducive to religious interpretation than the aforementioned theories for he has claimed that there seems to be a mystical element at work in language development. He claims that the mechanics of language must have more than a materialistic explanation to account for the refinement of multiple controls employed and there must be room left for this other element to operate. This leads to a much more responsive concept not only of language but also of the user of the infinite variation in language usage.

While there have been many developments that have thrown light on language usage as it reveals the deeper levels of the inner being, it is work with people that is most useful in showing what takes place in people. Not only does language work to obscure the deeper levels of the self from others but it is quite obvious that it keeps the person from awareness of what is going on in the depths of his own being. When persons have been indoctrinated with certain ideas they use those ideas as protection from doing their own thinking. They will tend to use those ideas uncritically instead of doing their own thinking. I served a church for a number of years in the suburbs of New York City where a number of the members were recent transplants from the deep south where much of the religious thinking was done by authoritarian preachers. They told people what to think and didn't encourage independent thinking. When personal crises developed I had the opportunity to work with them in personal counseling. I found that there was a certain amount of cut and dried thinking that took place that did not serve the counselee well in the current patterns of life. When I sought to throw them back on their own thought and feeling they were at first confused, for their traditional ways of thinking did not serve them well. They kept asking me what I thought and I did not feel that would be useful for them. When they finally were convinced that it was part of their mature meeting of crises to think them through for themselves they seemed to feel a new freedom. Though they might resent a nonauthoritarian approach at first, if they stayed with it they developed a new sense of freedom and personal adequacy that not only was essential to meeting the present crisis but was a useful resource for meeting others as well.

I have found that religious counseling as it has been practiced in the past has tended to confirm dependencies and trust of outside authorities and impede the development of true maturity. Since the process of counseling has been generally encouraged but as the teaching of crisis psychology has not yet been generally taught, many pastors have been more authoritative than was warranted and so the effective use of the discipline has been less than desired. This has shown up especially in the counseling that arises from family crises where pastoral experience is apt to get in the way of effective exploration of the deeper levels of the human factors that may be engaged.

As we have seen crisis psychology has depended on psychosomatic medicine for its basic material for research and on linguistics for its basic methodology. In a limited chapter such as this it is only possible to suggest the possibilities that lie in this new approach to pastoral care. Currently we look primarily to the past for our insights, but we must give ourselves increasingly to the possibilities that the future holds for innovative use of new research and methodology. That will require a shift in the emphasis of the education for pastoral intervention.

My own experience proved to be very important for directing me in my explorations. When in my first parish I had an assignment in a Veterans Administration Facility with 28 hundred shell-shocked veterans of the first World War. I realized quickly that the education I had received in seminary was irrelevant to that assignment and to any assignment when the persons were responding to stress. My three seminary years were focused on keeping alive a body of knowledge that was primarily centered on historical and biblical knowledge. There was very little knowledge about people in the curriculum. I soon recognized that I must supplement my education elsewhere.

At first I tried Yale where I was able to work out an arrangement where I could study communication in the Divinity School and social studies in the School of Human Relations. This provided a general background that met my needs and my three years there were very useful but I still needed the specifics and for that I enrolled in the Postgraduate Center for Psychotherapy. The faculty was made up primarily of medical doctors from the various medical schools in New York City. I was interested to discover that I was the only clergyman in the student body, which was made up largely of physicians and others who possessed advanced degrees. They were curious about my reasons for they assumed that pastors were authoritarians who were not really interested in knowing about people and what made them tick.

My three years working with physicians was useful to me for it filled in the lacking part of my education and confirmed my feeling that I could not minister to the whole person until I understood them in depth and could approach them with a nonjudgmental attitude of mind. Much of the seminary education I had received had worked against that kind of understanding. So I began a ministry to as many seminaries as would give me a hearing.

I found the student bodies at the 35 or so seminaries at which I regularly spoke actively interested in the depth dimension of communications with numerous questions about why their regular courses did not cover such vitally important subjects. Within recent years a number of seminaries have provided courses in their pastoral departments, primarily in hospitals, touching the matters of psychosomatics, but often those courses were overshadowed by the medical personnel who supervised them.

I believe I have had a positive influence on the seminary structure so that there is a more tolerant attitude toward those students who want to develop depth communication and the spiritual attitude toward true wholeness of being.

Among the students I found a desire to pursue my type of pastoral intervention through reading and advanced study and a number of them have worked on advanced degrees on related subjects and have on occasion asked me to work with them toward that end.

I know that curriculum revision is a constant process in a number of seminaries, but it is a slow process because the core subjects of the Bible, theology and church history are slow to relinquish their positions of status among the faculty. The subjects of communication and personality sciences take on a position of orphan children among the faculty.

As I look back over a half century of acquaintance with the seminary atmosphere, however, I am not discouraged for I see significant changes. Where some things were nonexistent when I started they have a vital place now. The forces at work to slow up the new movements are not all bad for they represent what has been learned from the past and we need that as a counter balance of the new and the uncertain. When I was invited to speak at a seminary in Chicago there was no class for everyone was attending a protest at a downtown rally but I understood for I had attended a lot of protests. It will take time and effort to bring about change in the climate of pastoral care and we are on the way. I hope that I have contributed my share to the new view of the church's role in ministering to the real needs of people.

Chapter 11

A METHODIST IN MY MADNESS

There are some words that carry a special meaning from such an early age that they are defined, often inadequately, by the very living of life. Such is the word Methodist in my life. My father and my paternal grandfather were both Methodist preachers and so the words were early associated with what was considered a worthy tradition. We have had fun trying to establish a relationship with John Wesley as if he were a patron saint. We have valued the unique qualities of his life but we have wondered if the rigid discipline of his own life and that he promulgated in the lives of others was necessarily a good thing for him and his followers. I have studied his life and the framework in which he was nurtured. In earlier years I read deeply into his letters and journals and I would often stub my mental toe upon ideas and practices that my study of psychotherapy would identify as morbid and unhealthy. Naturally I fitted them to their time and excused those things that seemed extreme as a product of their peculiar mindset. When Wesley remarked that he felt that only a handful of his pastors were so broken in spirit that they were completely subject to his will I felt that something was amiss in that relationship. It was obvious that what might have been acceptable two hundred years ago was not appropriate for this day. Neither my colleagues nor I would find that kind of relationship acceptable and when I encountered it or a reasonable facsimile I was bound to resist it. But I never thought it would happen to me as I went blissfully onward proud of the tradition in which I had been nurtured.

I remember spending a day in Wesley chapel in London from early morning throughout the day. The homily was by a prison chaplain and that was as it should have been for Wesley was deeply concerned about prisoners. He did not want them to be put to death for trivial crimes until they had made their peace with God. It was probably too early for thought about the social conditions that lead to the extremities of the penal system. I gloried in my own private apostolic succession that was started when John Wesley laid his hands on Francis Asbury who founded a church in 1771 that I served one hundred and eighty years later. During that time the laying on of hands was done by Peter Cartwright and my Grandfather completed the tie directly to John Wesley. I was proud of the fact that I was only three handshakes from the founder of my denomination. But it served no useful purpose when larger issues were confronted. My investment in fantasy served no purpose when a larger reality was at issue.

I knew that bishops under some conditions wielded great power over the persons who were subject to their appointive power. This was a power with the effect of life and death if it were applied ruthlessly. Down through the years the influence of a bishop to control those under his power was variously interpreted so that misuse was kept at a minimum. The act of ordination was administered in such a way that it implied that the ordinand was subject to a bishop as long as in the active ministry when the minister would go where he was sent with few questions asked. If they questioned they had to be satisfied with the answers or else they would have to take the consequences.

The conference is somewhat like a closed shop union for once admitted to the conference a person is guaranteed a parish assignment until retirement subject to certain limitations on conduct and health which have to be examined annually. Sometimes with changing conditions there are more pastors than churches so there may be forced retirements or a restriction on admissions. Recent years have seen a type of problem that sometimes arrived. Fifty percent of the graduates of some seminaries have been well-qualified women who seek admission to conferences but the conferences have not seemed ready to accept women as their senior pastors. Bishops have had to supervise the process of assignment of pastors during this period of transition and it is often complicated by social patterns and prejudice.

I was brought up under a regime of men who were out of the ordinary. The style of Bishop I admired and willingly followed was set by Francis J. McConnell, a man of superior intellect, maturity of personality and genuinely democratic. He was a keen student of personality and had respect for a human being because of his endowment. He treated everyone with deep respect and seemed to draw out the best in those he worked with because he expected only the best. I was invited to become the youth member of the board of trustees of the Methodist Federation for Social Service and accepted, for Bishop McConnell was the president and I could spend hours watching him preside. His graciousness as well as his perspicacity was a model for mature and competent behavior. We developed a close relationship. I entertained him in our home and accepted him as the model for a bishop's attitude and practice. I used him as a measure for every other bishop without realizing that he was the rare exception in every way.

I went merrily along in my ministry trying to follow the example of Bishop McConnell, as I perceived it. I took many positions of leadership in the conference, became the organizer and chairman of the pastoral care committee and was the only chairman of it as long as I was an active member of the conference. I was the only one who was ever Dean of the Conference summer program for four weeks during the summer season. I was a member of the board of education and the committee that supervised the ministerial relation with the conference. I was so heavily engaged in the many duties that I assumed for the conference that I felt I was neglecting the affairs of my own parish. I was also invited to assume a leadership role in the church at large, so I figured that I should reassess the investment of my time in the varied tasks I had assumed. I tried to decide what was important and give myself wholly to those tasks. So I withdrew from most of the conference assignments, especially those that I had held for many years. A good time to do that seemed to be when a new bishop was assigned to our conference. I did not realize that the new bishop might take the matter personally and that I might be embarking on a period of turbulence without any intent on my part.

I enjoyed studying people to see what made them tick. With my extensive study of psychology my understanding was facilitated. Because a bishop could become so important to a minister's career a careful study of their values, motivations and prejudices could prove to be relevant to many of life's judgments. When I started my exploration of the new bishop I was fortunate to be acquainted with people who could throw light on his life from early childhood. My study of childhood behavior and my experience of years as head of a state licensed psychiatric clinic for children and their parents were useful at this point. For instance, I found out that the favorite form of punishment by those responsible for his behavior as a child was to lock him in a dark closet until he cried himself into nervous exhaustion. The results of this form of treatment could be a nonrational reaction to any type of opposition for years to come. Under normal circumstances the impulse toward nonrational behavior might be controlled but in unusual circumstances it would be manifest in ways that showed an inability to function within the bounds of reason. The John Wesley pattern showed itself in the control of childhood behavior that led toward adult manifestations. The bishop seemed to be governed by such impulses often in his inability to deal with opposition rationally.

One of the Bishop's predecessors had appointed me to be the psychiatric counselor for members of the conference with gender identification issues and their spouses. Over a period of several years I had eighteen or twenty persons who were referred to me for such counseling and although I was no expert in such matters by experience and training I was not without some acquaintance with such problems and their management. I had hired a young man who was well-trained and capable. I had worked with him for two or three years when the Bishop asked me all sorts of personal questions about my associate. I answered all of them by saying that the subject had never arisen between us and his attitude and his work was always satisfactory from my point of view. The Bishop's suspicion and attitude toward my associate led him to accept a position as bank manager and the church lost a fine spirited and well qualified pastor. I considered the Bishop's interference unwarranted and felt that the church at large lost a good man because of it.

The Bishop, through his emissary, offered me some jobs that I did not want, but I was inclined to accept an offer that came from the University of Minnesota to serve as visiting professor teaching the new discipline of crisis psychology which I had pioneered through my writings in the psychological implications of psychosomatic medicine. I had written the first textbook in the field and I was interested in trying my wings at teaching if I could get away from my church without damaging the pastoral relationship. So I asked for a sabbatical year with the understanding that I would be returned to my parish at the end of the sabbatical. The Bishop tentatively agreed with the plan submitted by the pastoral committee of my parish. I turned over the furnished parsonage to the interim pastor and went my way.

I heard rumors of trouble from the parish but determined to keep hands off during the sabbatical year. I returned twice, once for a wedding and once for a committee making plans for the coming year. Some turbulence in the parish was brought to my attention but I said there would be time to care for that when I returned at the end of the year. I was sure that some changes had occurred but I had left a church at peace and growing in spirit and in grace and I did not think much of an adverse nature could have transpired in a year's absence. ·

Little did I know what could happen in a year when the effort was deliberate and far reaching. When I reported at the church office I was met by an apologetic church secretary who said she had been holding a letter that the interim pastor had directed her to send to every official of the church at once. It was a letter from the Bishop giving episcopal blessing to what the interim pastor had done. I read it with incredulity and told the secretary to hold everything until I had a chance to check on things. I spent the next few days conferring with officials and others about what had been happening. The parish had for years been run in a democratic manner with everyone being free to speak and everyone being treated with respect. The interim pastor was a retired district superintendent and seminary professor who was from Tennessee. He was well versed in early Methodism as Wesley was inclined to practice it. I had tried to recognize the needs of a community with many national and racial backgrounds, as you would expect in the region populated by many members of the United Nations. During the years I served as pastor I tried hard to make this into an interracial, international and interdenominational church and publicly declared it as such. As there was no other nonliturgical parish in the community it seemed the best way to serve the needs of the community. Everyone except some southern people who moved into the community seemed to approve the way the parish had developed. When some people of southern antecedents threatened to leave the church if I took in any more people of color I expressed regret but was willing to transfer their membership if so desired but felt that it was valid to explain in the letter of transfer the cause. When faced with the alternative, members invariably decided to remain with the church. The many hued congregation was, I felt, a triumph of the Christian spirit. But the interim pastor under the approval of the Bishop tried to remake what was in essence a community into a traditional southern Methodist church. When black persons tried to speak at an official board meeting the interim pastor openly insulted them and the parish was filled with turmoil.

It seemed that considerable effort was made to distort the understanding that was made concerning my personal possessions left in the parsonage. Some were sold at auction. Some were broken. My files were rifled and items were shared with the Bishop. It looked as if the year was used to bring my ministry into active conflict with the Bishop. His old friend, the interim pastor, violated our agreement and the normal courtesies with impunity and did all of these things without once communicating with me. I found out after my return that a committee of the parish had waited upon the Bishop to protest the damage the interim pastor was doing in the parish. The Bishop stonewalled and said that when he had spoken he had spoken. When I made an appointment to see the Bishop he stonewalled some more and said anything he had said or done was not subject to review and that I should get busy with the tasks of the parish to repair any damage I felt had been done. When I said that I felt my integrity had been damaged so that I could not continue to serve the parish or under his leadership he refused to discuss the matter and gave me no satisfaction. The hundred and twenty five years of active and honorable service to the conference by myself, my father and brother-in-law counted for nothing against his arrogance and intransigence. Nothing that could be done by me or the collective members of the parish was able to move the Bishop. I made it clear that I was not interested in a power struggle and was not intending any political action against him. As soon I said that he firmed up his position and disposed of me as one of his subjects without further ado. Several years later he did come to the lay leader of the parish and admitted that he had handled the whole matter badly and regretted his ineptness.

I continued to serve the parish throughout the year and asked for early retirement for which I had sufficient time already served. It is interesting that my colleagues in the conference with whom I had served for many years seemed satisfied with what had happened for there was no effort to support the strong claim I made for the sacredness of the role of the pastor in his parish. The Bishop had declared publicly that he would never interfere in the affairs of the local parish but my case was the exception to the rule. When my father sought to enter a senior citizens residence specially prepared for retired members of the conference he and my mother were denied entrance. The Bishop took action to see that it should never happen again but not retroactively.

I remember asking one of my friends who was an intimate of the Bishop how he explained the strange and irrational behavior of his friend the Bishop. He said that he thought it was explained by jealousy, pure and simple. He said that the Bishop was obviously disturbed by the prominence I had gained in the Methodist church as an author and lecturer. After the action of the Bishop against me I was in effect blackballed as far as lecture assignments across the church were concerned. I had taken a chance as far as income was concerned for my guaranteed salary from the parish was terminated, but the number of books in print and lectures from hospitals and universities piled up so that the income was the least of my worries. Freedom from parish duties gave me a whole new view of the possibilities of my professional life. I now traveled about the world telling of the relation of emotions to physical changes and, as I was on top of much research in psychosomatics, I was welcomed at medical schools and related fields of study. What I feared would be barren years until I was eligible for a pension were the most productive years of my life and without planning it, my Bishop became the best friend I ever had. His determination that I should face his stern judgment was the best thing that ever happened to me. Although I have missed the tradition and fellowship of the Methodist church, I have found a wider world in which to function and the freedom from restrictive administrative practices has been a blessing in disguise. Until I was hobbled by a crippling stroke in 1983, I had the best twenty years of my life. Although I had no supervision by a Bishop I had fifteen interim parishes in twenty years and enjoyed them all. Some were big, some were small but all gave me the chance to do the things I loved most, work with people, worship and deliver the message that seemed relevant. I guess I was always a preacher at heart and, if I had not been tripped up in midstream by a Bishop who used a church to work out his personality problems, I probably would have spent my career giving myself to parishes and people.

So you see I have had a chance to look at the Methodist Church from inside and out. I tried unsuccessfully to use my experience as a psychotherapist to clean up some of the unhappy traditions that were started by old John. I thought that it was a good thing but the church was not ready for it. But I had a good time trying and although I did not succeed I at least made an opportunity for an interesting and, I think, productive life. I think it is unfortunate for any opportunity for leadership to miscarry because of inadequate personality structure developed in childhood.

Chapter 12

MYSTICISM AND THE DEEPER REACHES OF PASTORAL CARE

During the past fifty odd years I have worked diligently in pastoral care. I believe that this phase of the pastor's function has greater importance and can be more functionally valid than other and more ephemeral aspects of the pastor's work. Some people, when introducing me to audiences, refer to me as one of the pioneers of modern forms of pastoral care. To be sure, my writing has been innovative in that I wrote the first book on the therapeutic function of preaching, the first book length psychological study of grief, the first text book on the new psychological discipline of crisis psychology and crisis management as well as the first book on parish counseling as a unique modality quite different from the clinical model of pastoral counseling as usually practiced. So over the years my basic interest in innovative methods in pastoral care has been well established.

During these years of pastoral work I grew increasingly restless as I perceived that the theological base from which I had been taught to operate was at sharp variance with the goals I set for pastoral intervention. I was seeking to encourage growth toward maturity and independence and at the same time was expected to teach dependence and promote a theological stance that promoted immaturity. I wanted to encourage people to think for themselves and develop their own inner genius and yet it was assumed that one could find salvation only by adhering to certain orthodox and traditional patterns of thought. I wanted to help people to discover an inner authority that could sustain life and achieve a philosophy of life adequate for all of life's circumstances, but I was expected to respond to external authority provided by a defensive and self-serving institution.

I sought to help people develop a loyalty to truth as a sound basis for living but found that I was expected to teach and encourage a framework of falsehood that was built into the system. I was seeking to teach inner peace and conciliation as a way of life, but found that on every side the institution that demanded loyalty fostered active conflict with other people and their ideas and projected an adversarial relationship upon the world.

In my work with people I sought to teach them to examine relentlessly the premises from which they operated in life but I found that the framework of ideas within which they were expected to operate personally was assaulted if they questioned certain irrational ideas that were taken for granted. All in all, I found that in my effort to teach openness and honesty with a respect for independent thinking and compassionate feeling, I was constantly thwarted by dogma and tradition.

I had the strong feeling that there must be a better theological base to operate from and I sought it. Basically I wanted it to have some of the authority and wisdom of the New Testament, some respect for the tradition that had been proven through long human experience, and a compatibility with the insights of contemporary science as far as psychology, anthropology, cosmology and philosophy were concerned.

I was fortunate in my commitment to the parish. My ministry had always been parish oriented. In fact the parish is the best laboratory for the study of people and their efforts to find religious answers to the important problems of life. The parish provides the opportunity to talk and work with people without raising the problems to the level of full consciousness. They are met in the spontaneity of their happening. The pastoral counselor has a more formal relationship with persons in its setting and arrangements. The parish setting has a kind of informality that allows people to reveal themselves with less restraint and more candor. Then too the pastor has more opportunities to encounter people and may be able to acquire a more accurate assessment of the total person. By meeting people in their own homes the pastor is able to evaluate many facets of life rather than the one that is presented in the more formal setting where the pastoral counselor is presiding.

In over fifty years of pastoral ministry I have run into every kind of situation. The pastoral ministry is filled with all sorts of human problems and opportunities. The pastoral person has always had the advantage of being able to meet people where they are most themselves, in the home. The most advanced types of counseling, conjoint family therapy and the social work interview, are usually done in the home setting. The pastor is the person who can reach the distressed individual first and in the most natural setting and therefore may be most effective. The pastor does not have to wait for the parishioner to take the initiative but may use any sensitivity or awareness possible to start the process of moving toward an injured person.

Wayne Oates in a published review of one of my books commented on the authenticity of my case material. It was taken directly from parish experience and though it was carefully disguised to protect the identity of the people involved, it was usually the way it happened. A professor of Christian Education lived in our home for two weeks to study the parish program in preparation for writing the book <u>These Parishes are Succeeding</u>. In it he quoted the members of my parish as saying "he seems to have the knack of always being there when we need him most". I think that was so because I made an effort to see and understand their needs and struggles and to meet those needs. Sometimes that is easier than others. I made it a practice to be with them in court, in the hospital and when there were family crises such as fires. Being present at such times was an immediate vent for emotion and provided reassurance when it was most valid.

When I delivered a manuscript to Jason Aronson who was one of my publishers after he had had an initial reading of a book on a philosophy for parish management he queried me in detail. As he was by profession a psychotherapist and trained as a psychoanalyst he was particularly interested in the nature of my encounter with the parishioners. Comparing my method with psychoanalysis he admitted that he did not know there was such a method for rapid movement in treatment. I responded that it was implicit in the parish context. As a Psychoanalyst, he would never say 'hello' to a patient in the elevator lest he contaminate the relationship. I said I related to people in their homes, their places of business, recreation, worship and most of the other places of life. If I am constantly observant I have a multifaceted way of knowing them and their way of thinking and acting long before I have occasion to start a counseling process so that much of the work is already well begun before the counseling session begins. I have long been of the opinion that parish centered counseling is a unique modality and have tried to develop that idea in my book <u>Parish Counseling</u>. In its method and in its practice it is able to create conditions of encounter that are not found in any form of therapeutic encounter commonly practiced. For that reason its uniqueness should be developed rather than manipulated into other forms of relationship that produce a hybrid that has a negative of both of the sources of the hybridized methods.

Another matter that is of major importance is the basic philosophy that is employed in parish-centered counseling. I was convinced that the pastor in the parish was equipped with resources that were lacking in most other types of psychotherapy. First among these was a theological perspective that was of major importance in all that was said and done. The pastor makes working assumptions about the nature of a human being that give a positive quality to the encounter that is being engaged in. A person is worth living and dying for and so the quality of the investment with that person is guaranteed. This is quite a different assumption than that entered into in a merely professional relationship.

Second, the person has a right to pastoral care without thought of remuneration or financial obligation. The pastor's salary is provided by the church and is guaranteed without regard to any other stipulations that may be made. I like this freedom that protects the relationship with the counselee and is limited to the two parties in the counseling process

Third is the institutional connection, for you are never working alone. You are always backed up by a church, which has a history, a body of beliefs, traditional practice and a structure of actions that make up its life. It has a viable entity actively and passively and has a personality and presence that can be counted on to back up individual practices and convictions. It has both a corrective and guarantor of social stability always available to those who give it allegiance.

Fourth, there is an assumption constantly at work in the pastoral role that is accepting and nonjudgmental. People in crisis have a deep need to be accepted by someone who is seeking to understand them and approach them free from damaging attitudes and presuppositions. I have had many counselees who have commented upon the freedom of our counseling relationship from their expected judgment and predisposition toward preaching. These four qualities that tend to mark modern pastoral relationships go far toward setting the new boundaries within which the pastoral role is cast. But the role is blurred by the impressions that are made by fundamentalists and eclectic media that see the pastoral role in a way that has long been outlived. I have found it wise to carefully describe the boundaries within which I expect to work and within which I expect counselees to function. This frees up the relationship from all sorts of false assumptions about the processes that relate pastor and people.

One of the more ancient and honored modes of pastoral intervention has been that provided by the pastoral guide or spiritual director. In an age where pastoral responsibilities have been tinged by clinical disciplines and bounded by a philosophy that has been developed from psychological and clinical perceptions, it may well be that some of the rich elements of the pastoral tradition have been allowed to wither away or become so completely amalgamated with other modes of thinking and acting that some of the important perceptions of the tradition have been vitiated.

It is the intent of this chapter to look carefully at the role of the spiritual guide; to assess the dynamics of process employed, evaluate its meaning in contemporary pastoral practice and assess the role, if any, which this ancient and traditional form of pastoral practice may have in the emerging philosophy of pastoral care.

Four sources of insight will be brought into focus. First, is a feeling of dissatisfaction with the philosophical base from which much of modern pastoral intervention proceeded; second, is a body of experience developed over the past eighteen years in pastoral encounters as a spiritual guide; third, a fortunate discovery of a body of literature that illuminates the role of the spiritual guide; and fourth, a helpful critique of my experience by competent and qualified practitioners of pastoral care in its contemporary format.

In my book The Pastor And His People I used the introductory chapter to define a pastoral stance that would be both biblical and nonmanipulative. In my book Parish Counseling I elaborated on this approach to counseling emphasizing the unique and powerful relationship that potentially existed between a pastor and a person in a parish. I am now working on a Theology For Parish Care which I trust will develop more fully the concepts of God, person and process that can bring together the rich insights of the personality sciences and the profound and unique resources resident in the pastoral person. Space limitations will make it impossible to develop that relationship fully in this chapter but it will be hinted at occasionally and will be implicit constantly.

Through years in the parish ministry I was constantly aware of the limitations on time which the many faceted task thrust upon me. In the eighteen years since retirement there has been ample time to keep persons in focus and stay with them through the dark nights of the soul when they were struggling to discover the essentials of selfhood and the relationship of the cosmic source of being. During these years I have spent hundreds of hours with a selected group of persons, often in academic pursuits, but more often in silence and meditation as the frontiers of being were gently pushed back to reveal the essence of being and cosmic relationship. Here the quest was primarily for wisdom and understanding rather than knowledge, and the method was to stimulate the growing edge of being by the appropriate question rather than providing answers themselves. An actual encounter will illustrate the process.

Any process that moves deeply into the subjective calls for benchmarks to test and check the validity of the process. So in the third place I have valued the hours of discussion I have had with counselors, spiritual guides and professors of pastoral care who have evaluated, criticized and appreciated methods and goals of this form of pastoral care. Some of these valid assessments will appear as we proceed in our exploration. Like any other form of human encounter, many variables exist and the end results are dependent on objective and subjective forces that may be at work. No two encounters are the same or even comparable though they move with common interests toward shared goals.

Perhaps the joy and fascination of serving as a spiritual guide or director is the wonder of the human dimension in all of its subtle variations for both the guide and the pilgrim discover new depths of meaning in themselves and each other as they take the time to share a common path from where they were to where they seek to be. In a relationship of sublime trust with no commercial overtones the self discovers ever deeper layers of being which may not have been surmised until they are discovered by the patient and penetrating resonance to each other that the shared experience makes possible.

Let us look at an actual encounter to see what took place and how it happened. Certain superficial information is modified to protect the sacredness of this form of privileged communication.

It happened this way. One day in the morning's mail there was a letter that said in part, "I have read your book on understanding prayer. It made sense to me and I would like to talk with you about it. I have many questions still unanswered. I can meet you most anywhere. I am a pilot for an airline that goes to many of the cities in our country. I can usually adjust my schedule. Please call me and I am sure we can work things out if you would be interested."

As I travel far and wide and often it was easy for me to arrive at a city a day ahead of my scheduled engagement and meet at an airport motel to spend the better part of a day in a leisurely encounter with a limited agenda. Rooms were adjacent so there was time to be together as well as alone, for it is an important part of the process to have time for meditation and the digesting of thoughts and feelings.

So it was that I met Barry Curtis, tall, slim and in his middle thirties. For years people had come to me with problems, so by tradition I had looked for signs of their disturbance so that I might more readily explore with them their areas of stress. Not so with Barry who appeared to be calm and self-possessed. When we first met at the baggage claim area in Minneapolis he expressed his thanks for my willingness to meet him and said that he had checked in at the motel an hour or so earlier. We agreed to meet for lunch in an hour.

In a quiet corner of a nearly empty dining room we began to talk. I suggested that he probably had his personal agenda and that I would be glad to know what it was. His opening gambit was cautious yet candid. He said, "I'm living a good life but I feel there should be more to it. I'm glad to be a pilot but take-off and landing are hardly enough to satisfy me. I have always had a spiritual feeling for life, but it has always been rather inarticulate,—unfocused. I read your book and it began to bring some things together, but not enough to satisfy me. So here I am and here you are."

"Good. Now where would you like to go?"

"Well, that's part of the problem. I know I have an inner life, but I don't know much about it. It always seems just out of reach. It doesn't seem to do me much good because it is never quite real. It never seems to be my own."

"How so?"

"Well, I don't know how to explain it. I read a lot. The books all seem to talk about a powerful force that can be at work. I believe that because so many people say so, but it never seems to come alive for me. It is a potential but not an actual."

So it was that Barry marked out the area he wanted to explore. How could he discover the fuller nature and resource of his inner being?

We spent more than four hours that afternoon, three more that evening and three more the next morning talking together about Barry's feelings about himself and his life. Much of it was autobiographical, not so much externals as internals. He had always wanted to be a doctor and in college he had taken a predominantly scientific course. One of those international stress points had occurred and he had been induced to enlist in the Air Force. He was trained as a pilot, the war ended and he was surplus so applied to a major carrier and was soon regularly employed as a pilot. During the ensuing ten years he had married happily and had three young children. Externally life seemed to be going well but internally there were restlessness and a searching, what often is referred to as a mid-life crisis. As he articulated the elements of this mid-life quandary there seemed to be three things that bothered him. One was the unfinished business of his high school idealism. Another was an effort to reconcile his scientific insight with his spiritual sensitivity. Third was an expressed need to go back over what he knew about religion to see if it could be brought together in a valid and useful construct for he had the feeling that there was more there than his past attitudes and practice had made accessible to him.

His earlier vocational choice, being a physician, had satisfied an idealistic component in his life. He wanted to be useful and help people in a dramatic way. Being a pilot, or as he put it "a glorified bus driver" did not fit the basic requirements of his idealistic nature. The glamour of the vocation had worn thin and he was not entirely satisfied with himself. He wondered if there was some way of combining the two vocations. As we explored it he indicated that he felt he had healing in his hands and that on several occasions people had said that they felt benefits from his touch. As he had read about "laying on of Hands" he wondered if this might be the way he could recover a sense of a valued vocation. We agreed that it would be important for him to do some deeper study of the subject before our next session together. I suggested that he read books by Morton Kelsey, John McNeill and Charles Kemp dealing with the history of healing in the church. Also I said I would send him a manuscript copy of my book which was published subsequently under the title The Role Of Faith In The Process Of Healing. As an avid reader with lots of time on his hands these assignments were eagerly accepted.

He indicated that he had been quite religious in his earlier life but had found an active conflict between what he was taught in the church and in science classes in the university. He had found the sciences more satisfying and had let go of his religion. But now he was concerned because the methods of science seemed to exclude so much of life from careful study. He had been reading Pierre Teilhard and was confused by it for there seemed to be more there than he was getting. Here I suggested he explore Carrel, Sinnott, Burtt, Polanyi and Maslow.

On the matter of basic religion he had done some reading on meditation and its benefits but felt some of it was so "kooky" that he was uncomfortable with it. In response to his queries we pointed out some of the books on prayer and the spiritual life that might prove useful like LeShan, and classics like Underhill and Von Hugel.

Barry was a person of disciplined intellect and a questing spirit. He was willing to work diligently in his search. I did not want to manipulate his exploration but I did want to help him find what could be useful for him without limiting the free movement of his mind and spirit. I respected his basic endowment so much that I did not want to manipulate him. Rather I sought to facilitate the growth he was comfortable with.

I checked my travel schedule and we agreed to meet for a day in Seattle two months hence. We parted with a feeling of personal warmth at the stimulation of our common quest. We had become spiritual friends.

When we met in Seattle we stayed at Barry's home and shared some of our time with his family. This added another dimension to our explorations. Barry's wife was a devout Roman Catholic who had tried to avoid any pressure upon him and his now nominal Protestantism. During the two months time between our sessions he had read Morton Kelsey, who because of his Notre Dame connection had been assumed to be Roman Catholic. We clarified that. Also he had read Carrel and Teilhard.

For several hours we explored his reading and his reactions to what he had read. He proved to be an avid reader with excitement generated by exploring new horizons. Kelsey gave him a new perspective on the long exploration of healing in the history of Christendom, with a greater appreciation of human concern about health and the mysterious processes that have always been present even when efforts at a more exact science have motivated medicine.

Yet his concern was not so much with history as it was with methods of healing and the techniques to be employed. So we spent some time exploring the transcribed reports of the Wainwright seminars of spiritual healing where physicians, psychologists and practitioners of the spiritual dimension of healing shared their insights and compared their observations and experiences. This directed the reading and research in a new direction, more practical than theoretical. Arrangements were made to send Barry the full set of transcripts of the seminars for future examination. Then Barry said that he had long felt a desire to lay hands on people. He had read about it and yet was timid about doing it. He reported that he often felt an urge to intervene when people said they had headaches or muscular pains. However, he was not sure enough of himself or of the process to assume initiative. So we explored the meaning of the process and the feelings that would be related to it. Having engaged in the laying on of hands at least twenty five thousand times, I suggested that we try it. First I stood behind the chair on which he was sitting and placed my hands gently on his shoulders above the major nerve center there. After a few minutes we took time to assess his feelings.

Barry talked freely about his feelings, both subjective and objective. He indicated that he had expected something more dramatic and perhaps startling. Instead he said he felt a warming sensation with a quieting and peaceful feeling throughout his being. He said he would like to sit quietly for a time to try to consolidate his feelings of tranquility. He closed his eyes and breathed deeply for a while. After a few minutes of quiet contemplation he responded that it was a good feeling, hard to explain but that he would like to feel that way more often. He said it was as if stress were melting away as if something deep within himself were being activated and he was trying to discover what it was that was really happening inside of him.

Barry's fascination with the process of healing had many dimensions. There was a fulfillment of adolescent interest and his early vocational choice. There was also a mystical interest in putting many things together in new arrangements. There was a desire for new and meaningful experience. He asked if he could try his hands at the process and I willingly assented to his request. Taking some time to prepare himself he cautiously placed his hands on my shoulders and held them there for a few minutes. When he tried to evaluate his feelings in this action he claimed a strong feeling of relationship. He said that he hadn't ever touched another human with spiritual intent and he wondered about the differences in touching that might be involved.

This experience led to a lengthy discourse on relationship and the role of the skin. He said that off and on through his life since adolescence he had been troubled by a skin rash that came and went and for which there seemed to be no medical explanation or effective treatment. He free-associated at some length about his inner being and its relationship to the outside world through the agency of his skin. This brought into focus a great deal of experience that had to do with other people, touching in its many forms through eye, ear, tongue, olfactory sense as well as sexual behavior. He admitted that since childhood he had been quite reserved about matters of touching. He began to wonder about what life had done to him in the touching department. He recalled that after his birth his mother had suffered from a long illness. He wondered if that had had anything to do with some of his basic characteristics. During this time of contemplation there were long periods of silence as he explored his memory and his consciousness. This exploration of skin, touching and human relationships took up the time of the day we had planned to be together, and he was intent upon following up on the meaning of skin and its relationship to communication.

In about ten weeks I was to be in Oklahoma City and Barry arranged to meet me there with about a day's time to share. We set up some reading assignments on the physiology of skin and the senses. I recommended exploring Ashley Montague's book on touching as well as Dolores Krieger's training manual for nurses, Therapeutic Touch. A major change in emphasis had emerged in Barry's thinking during this session. From a purely intellectual interest in the relation of mind and body he had begun to focus his attention on actual behavior and the meaning of this broader aspect of human relationships. He appeared to be just as actively interested in the objective processes as he had been in the more subjective spurred by his previous reading. Without much specific guidance he moved more deeply into the exploration of relationship between himself and his intellectual interests.

When we met at the Oklahoma City airport Barry was primed for a lot of exploration. He had read extensively on the physiology of skin and its primacy as the boundary between the inner and outer being. Also he was intrigued by the importance of touching, and had brought together some interesting insights. He said it was quite obvious that there were at least three major types of touching, physical or sensual touching, intellectual touch where a caring perception of another could give a therapeutic quality to human touch. Then he felt there was a spiritual form of touching that was employed in the laying on of hands. After an afternoon session that lasted four hours he suggested we spend some time in meditation and the laying on of hands. He seemed to feel more relaxed and comfortable with this process than he had in our earlier session. Barry said that his experience of recent weeks had brought interesting changes to his relationship with his wife and children.

We talked about the meaning of relationship to a church. I told him about my experience working in the Vatican and my time teaching in a Benedictine seminary. We looked at the superficial meaning of the church to many of its adherents and the deeper meaning often observed. We talked of Teilhard and his experience. The decision had to be his and

I trusted him to make this step on his spiritual journey with wisdom and with confidence in its meaning for his life.

Before we had a chance to meet next he wrote and said he had been assigned an overseas route and would not be able to keep up the schedule planned. He was more than gracious and said that our sessions had produced important changes in his life and had gone a long way toward helping him to remake his life closer to his heart's desire.

He indicated that his feelings toward his wife had deepened as he invested them with more meaning. His wife had new depths in her being involved in their relationship and they enjoyed each other more. This was true in that they listened to each other more carefully. They were actually surprised to find how much more there was in their relationship to be explored. There was a new sense of wonderment in their lives as well as in their children's lives. These new dimensions were talked about with great interest. In fact it seemed to Barry that life was becoming a new experience all around.

We spent the evening and next morning exploring the meaning of what was happening from various points of view. There was a deep interest in knowing all there was to know about these new experiences in life and human relations. There was also an expression of caution and mild apprehension lest what was happening might need to be looked at from the negative side. The state of euphoria was so overwhelming that it carried its own sense of threat. So we talked at great length about it. It was important to think about the deeper meaning of what was happening. We talked about the importance of grounding energy. The principle applied to spiritual as well as other forms of life experience. He had used the uncertainty of his employment to avoid any commitments to his family as religious activity. Now he raised some questions as to whether it was important or not. We parted with unresolved questions. He gave me his future schedule and agreed to meet in Kansas City about two months hence.

In KC Barry said that he had talked with his wife about the matter of grounding and that he had decided to join the Catholic Church. He had waited to talk with me first. I said that his actions were his own and I did not want to influence him one way or the other.

I have used this shorter case because it illustrates the method without undo length. It is a privileged relationship that develops when one works as a spiritual guide. It takes training and is demanding of time and effort but it provides rewards that are special. I have never taken money for this privileged relationship. It is a part of ministry and should be kept free of the more mundane elements of life. It is a time for developing and practicing the mystical dimension of the ministry and one of the blessings of retirement is to be able to invest time so generously. The work of the spiritual guide may well be the highest form of pastoral work and often the most rewarding of its many forms.

1
2
4
3

1.Edgar Starkey and Abbie Newman Jackson with their 2 oldest sons.
2. Abbie and Edgar N.
3. Edgar at one year
4. Edgar 1927 H.S. Senior Picture

1934 Wedding Edgar and Estelle

1934 Honeymoon

Early marriage photo (undated)

Edgar S. and Abbie Jackson
leaving Bridgeport Church in 1946

Author photos 1960s and '70s

Chaplain U.S. Army Air Corps

James and Lois Photos

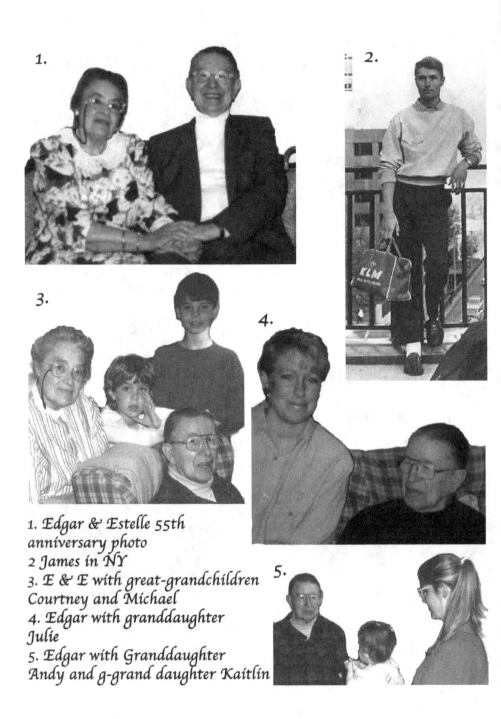

1. Edgar & Estelle 55th
anniversary photo
2 James in NY
3. E & E with great-grandchildren
Courtney and Michael
4. Edgar with granddaughter
Julie
5. Edgar with Granddaughter
Andy and g-grand daughter Kaitlin

Edgar preaching in
Mamaroneck Methodist
Church 1962

Edgar receiving award from New England Institute 1979

Chapter 13

MYSTICISM AND PAIN

I have been pretty well convinced that a person's attitude of mind has considerable bearing on the way that person functions. After I read Flanders Dunbar's book <u>Emotions and Bodily Changes,</u> I was always on the lookout for evidence of the processes by which these changes occurred and often the feelings that seemed to be involved. One of my physician friends pointed out that many of my interventions were marked by a reduction of pain and as many of their observations were related to their own experience it seemed quite reasonable to think that they knew their own feelings and so knew what they were talking about.

Pain has long been a factor in influencing the behavior of others. The whole psychology of punishment has been filled with administering of pain, physical or mental, to modify the behavior of others. Pain with purpose has a long history. We see it used in animal behavior when the jockey applies the whip in order to get the last ounce of speed from his mount during the final seconds of a race.

Many questions arise as we look at the use of pain in relation to the modifying of pain. What are the states of consciousness that are affected by pain? How can these same states of consciousness be modified so that pain is reduced or in some instances removed completely? What is the relationship of pain, physical or mental, to consciousness? What is the special state of perception called the mystical awareness as it relates to the experience of pain? How can the person whose awareness is centered on pain discover ways of modifying sensory acuity so that it will make it possible to modify the experience of pain? These are some of the questions that come to mind as we assess the subject.

At the beginning we have to ask ourselves some other basic questions. What is the function of pain? If we obliterate pain artificially do we threaten the purpose of pain? When and how do psychological states enhance pain? Why does theology raise pain to a cosmic dimension? What are the mental and emotional states that can be achieved to reduce the awareness of pain? Is there such a thing as pain without purpose?

It has long been assumed that pain is a signal. When the physical organism is made aware of danger or threats through pain, the sensation is not only a signal of hazard but also a stimulus to intervene to seek relief. When the rare condition exists that a child is born without the nerve formation that can be aware of pain, this child is faced with special hazard and may suffer severe burns or other injuries because the ability to be warned of danger has not been available to educate the child concerning the cause effect relationship between the experiencing self and the hazardous environment.

When pain exists it is important for the practitioner to know just where it is and how intense it is. Also it helps to know the way pain can show up in remote parts of the body far from the assumed causal area. So the physician probes to focus on pain producing tissues. This is impor-

141

tant for the tasks of diagnosis and prescription. We live in a time when there has been a considerable development of chemical agents that are available to modify and manage physical distress. One of the evidences that we can build a better world through chemistry is seen in the effort to provide a pill for every pain. Then we must caution against chemical abuse. We must ask ourselves the relevant questions such as what is the meaning of such modification of consciousness? Is it helpful to interfere with or modify the pain sensing equipment? What is the psychological effect of this form of pain management? Does it do harm to the individual to modify consciousness chemically to alleviate the symptoms of organic malfunction?

Much of the history of religion has been built about the cause-effect factors that effected pain and suffering. We do not study these processes long before we become aware that humankind seeks to find cosmic dimensions for the application of and the relief from pain. The discovery of anesthetics was greeted by a theological response. The assumption was that if pain were eliminated there would be no means of controlling behavior. When it was possible through medical advancement to relieve the pain of childbirth this was considered to interfere with the original sin of sex and to meddle with the Divine order. When experiments in the management of mental processes through hypnosis were tried, these efforts to control, understand, and manipulate the inner beings of a person were considered an unwarranted interference with the sacred precincts of self. It was condemned as witchcraft. Dire consequences were predicted for both practitioners and patients of this dark art.

The theological conflict about pain seems now to have been resolved in the direction of compassion. Few think unlimited pain serves any useful purpose for God or human. Yet echoes of the past rear their ugly heads in the current discussion of AIDS.

The focus of research can move in more than one direction. We can explore the control of consciousness by chemical agents or by the manipulation of mental and emotional resources. Let us look briefly at how these directions manifest themselves.

The most popular form for modifying organic stress in our day is through use of chemical agents. Each year thousands of tons of sedation, tranquilizers and pain relievers such as aspirin are used to modify consciousness. Contrary to usual medical practice, which hesitates to use a drug without knowing how it works aspirin and other such drugs are used even though little is known of their function in the body. Petrie says it seems to be used primarily to change a person from an augmenter to a reducer. It appears that the basic consciousness of the individual becomes a major determinant of the effectiveness of drug therapy. The chemical modification of consciousness is dependent for its effect on already existing internal determinants. This may well be why Petrie concludes: "he who is least susceptible to deprivation is most susceptible to pain and vice versa".

So we might conclude that, both consciously and unconsciously, those who would use external stimuli or chemical agents are more dependent upon internally determined degrees of perception than they realize for the effects they observe. This would lead us to examine more closely the second alternative of our explanation at this point. The internal mechanisms that bear on the experience of pain may point in the direction that can modify pain, free from some of the side effects of the chemically ingested agents. For if the chemistry is ultimately dependent upon the quality of consciousness, it may make sense to examine the nature of that internal state of being to understand its effect upon pain.

It is one of the common experiences of people that they move from a state of pain into a state of painlessness when they go to sleep. This perhaps is our most common form of modification of consciousness. We all engage in it as part of every day. What are the mechanisms operative to cause the change from pain to painlessness by moving from one state of awareness to another?

143

The religious consciousness has usually worked to create a type of psychic awareness which eases the pains of life and gives calmness, peace and internal release from the stresses that may cause pain and suffering. Religious groups have always been interested in healing in one form or another. Often this approach to healing has employed a modification of consciousness and a change in focus for awareness. Often this also uses social processes and ceremonial activities that help to modify psychic states. The mood that is created may be referred to as the mystical perception.

The mystical consciousness may be cultivated in several ways and the form employed may be closely related to tradition and learned modes of behavior. For instance, in Western thought the premise for moving into the mystical sensitiveness has been a cultivation of the rational as a springboard into the mystical state of being. Some of the great mystics of the Western tradition have also been prominent scientists. We might mention Pascal, Swedenborg, Bergson, Einstein and Teilhard De Chardin as typical. Here the mystical was an overflow of the rational, a form of psychic overdrive where the consciousness took off for higher forms of awareness. Humanist psychologists are deeply concerned in exploring this dimension of human experience. Yet always the starting point seems to be the rational for we would seek understanding of the process at the same time that we would experience its spiritual meaning.

In recent years the study of psychology and the nature of mental processes has helped us to move a step closer to some answers to the questions of pain, mysticism, and the use and modification of consciousness to control the physical sensations of the body.

The study of heightened perception and the mystical awareness has followed several lines of investigation. There are those who have sought practical and usable answers in their research.

On the other hand the Zen tradition sought the mystical awareness in freedom from the demands of the purely rational. The Zen master con-

144

fronted his disciples with deliberate efforts to affront the rational. The assumption seemed to be that the mystical awareness would be found not at the point of the contrived and purposeful but rather at the point where man's mental manipulations were left far behind and the impulse of powerful feelings and a cosmic awareness would combine to produce the flights of fancy that would produce the transpersonal illumination.

If these three types of mystical quest seem strange to our way of thinking it may help us to understand that they are all well and alive in our contemporary social structure. The humanistic psychologists and main line religious groups who seek mystical awareness usually tend to do so through the use of rational approaches and forms of discipline. Those who feel that the mystical can only be released by a denial of the rational are more apt to be found among groups of fundamentalists or the Pentecostals who are suspicious of learning and hostile to dependence upon reason. And those who would seek a mystical awareness through theoretical non-materiality are represented by the Christian Scientists who claim that material is illusory and that by practicing a theoretical denial they can create the means of mystical power to be employed in life to control disease and pain.

However, in recent years of the study of psychology, the nature of mental processes has helped us to move a step closer to some answers to the problems of pain, consciousness and mysticism, and the use and modification of the physical sensations of the body.

The study of heightened consciousness has followed several lines of investigation. Some parapsychologists have used scientific forms of measurement. Some have tried to understand the philosophical approach to understanding behavior. The research of Dr. LeShan is a good example of the effort to understand and manage states of consciousness for specific and practical use. He sought to relate and correlate the emotional state of an individual to the development of the neoplastic tissue in that individual. Changes in the emotional state appeared to produce changes in the physical state. Chronic emotional states appeared to produce chronic stress on the endocrine system's ability to satisfy bodily needs, which in turn reduced the body's ability to manage the effects of acute stress. This chemical imbalance appeared to allow abnormal cell division, which in turn allowed viral developments to be out of control. These processes when out of control appear to be related to the growth of malignant tissue.

Since childhood and my work with my aunt Dorothy I have been vitally interested in cancer and its causes. Now this study of emotional behavior and the onset of neoplastic disease was a clear cause-effect relationship to be explored in detail. If this development could be explored in one direction it was logical to think it could as well be explored in reverse. If disturbed states of consciousness could be followed in one direction they could as well be followed in the opposite direction. The control of body chemistry could as well control the development of the neoplastic cells and tissue.

In my work with Dr. LeShan we tried to trace back the causative factor to see if it would produce what has been called a spontaneous regression. If we could find a key to the regression we would take a step toward resolving the mysterious process at work in cancer. If disturbed states of consciousness could cause chemical imbalance in the body, it was reasonable to believe that the restoration of emotional balance within the person could produce an advantageous effect upon the body chemistry in the opposite direction.

In psychotherapeutic intervention this seemed to be the case and there was a correlation between spontaneous regressions and the emotional states of individuals. Where the "bleak and unutterable" despair remained there was little change in the neoplastic development. However, when it was possible to modify the content of consciousness deep within, there was likelihood of the change in body chemistry that seemed to be the physiological base for the so-called spontaneous regression.

If this change in the content of consciousness could be used to change the inner balance of the body, it seemed logical as a next step, that this change was something that could be learned and developed. Not only could a person be led to modify the content of consciousness, but methods could be learned where it could be possible for people to help each other in the process through support groups. A more healthful emotional climate for the healing process could be deliberately created. People could be trained to be partners in the healing process.

Central in this learning experience was the training of mental processes so that they were significantly altered and the equivalent of the mystical sensitivity was achieved. Where doubt and fear existed, this form of psychic artificial respiration seemed to be able to stimulate faith and courage. A new internal climate emerged which was more responsive to the natural stimulus of the healing process.

We have observed that the altered state of consciousness achieved in this learning process is quite comparable to the mystical state as usually perceived. The product of the clinical process appears to be quite like that achieved in the psychically controlled healing process and the mystically controlled states of heightened sensitivity.

This observation seems to be further supported by the careful work being done to understand the emotional dynamics and physiological processes that are employed in the effort to understand how the altered states of consciousness are involved in the healing process. Here the insights of Alyce Greene and her husband Elmer of the Menninger Clinic and William Johnson of the Jesuit Teaching Center in Tokyo have been most helpful.

For decades it has been most useful diagnostically for physicians to measure the brain waves of patients and the cycles in which they move. These cycles have been explored to understand their relation to the experience of pain. The observations seem to have an active relationship to traditional and mystical states of consciousness as far as they are employed to modify the registration of brain waves. The brain waves are classified as follows: O to 4 is delta, 4 to 8 is theta, 8 to 12 is alpha, and 12 to 20 is beta. The area of waking consciousness is recorded in beta. This is where the whole battery of sensory awareness is experienced. Delta and theta are usually the brain cycles manifested in sleep. Alpha represents the area of consciousness between the normal states of waking and sleeping. In the alpha cycle there is an ability to remain conscious and at the same time reduce or eliminate certain forms of sensory awareness.

The Greene findings indicate that if a person masters the techniques for moving into alpha cycles it is possible in many instances to control and perhaps completely eliminate the painful symptoms of migraine headaches.

At this point it is interesting to note the correspondence between alpha awareness and traditional forms of meditation. Almost always in prayer a person closes the eyes and may be so deeply in concentration that he reduces sound and other forms of sensory intrusion. In prayer groups it has been a common experience that during periods of deep prayer members of the group experience temporary disorientation when they try to return to normal waking consciousness.

In our essentially sensate culture it seems inevitable that the full sensory awareness undiluted by any alpha involvement would predispose persons to an intensification of any of the stimuli that are pain inducing. For that reason it seems desirable to cultivate and discipline the other cycles of awareness so that the incidence of pain could be ameliorated. In other words, the development of the ability to experience the mystical consciousness may be an important discipline for our culture to achieve. It could well reduce the dependence upon chemical forms of intervention to modify pain.

But the practical and physiological ventures into the understanding and control of the types of awareness that have long been identified as mystical cannot be left in the realm of techniques and manipulations without hazard. One of the serious problems of much of the research in the levels of consciousness in the past century has been that it was often unrelated to any adequate philosophical base. The clinical observation was extensive but the inadequate base tended to make meaning of the meaningless, and distort a technique into a form of philosophical meaning.

Increasingly those who have an interest in the mystical level of awareness and its varied benefits should be building their observations and experiences upon a structure of cosmic assumptions that are important enough to give both direction and validity to what we learn about consciousness in its natural and modified states. This places an emphasis on communication. Viewed in this sense the whole structure of being, body, mind and spirit is in communication constantly and so there is what could be called intrapsychic balance and homeostasis, or equilibrium among the communicating parts. Then it is seen that disease is a breakdown of relationship and pain is the message that is broadcast when the inner relationships are overburdened by stress or fractured by distortions of being.

Such a philosophical awareness tends to bring into focus the meaning of psychic and organic behavior in such a way that we may be able to objectify them and so bring about psychic and organic changes.

Central in the mystic discipline for the modification of consciousness is the quest for inner singularity or oneness of being. The mystic moves into the self to separate the being from the distractions that may be leading to stress and breakdown—the decentralization of being. He seeks to move beyond the distraction messages that flood consciousness with sensory awareness, to find the central meaning that brings into focus the communications of the being with the multiplicity of beings at work within the self.

These beings are psychological, accidental and cosmic. The release from pain through the mystical disciplines appears to be effective at all levels. The disciplined spirit can not only control the mechanisms of the body, and the qualities of the mind but also the unity with the cosmic that brings control of the spiritual processes of life.

It is this interpretation that had led George Mahoney, a Jesuit priest, to make a long and careful study of the mysticism of the East. Mahoney writes, "Christianity believes that man was meant by his Creator to soar like a bird into the upper reaches of their rarefied spiritual atmosphere through his power of knowing and loving; That most western Christians need some new methods for praying, in a deeper, more personalized level, is hardly to be disputed; Teilhard de Chardin was saying the same thing when he remarked that humanity today must choose between worship and suicide." "A developing Christian Yoga must assist the individual toward interior silence, toward unification and purification of body and soul, and toward a consciously realized surrender of the part into the whole. To be such a contemplative means ultimately to become a fully realized human being. Hindu and Eastern Orthodox mystics have much to teach western Christians about this."

So we have come full cycle through the practical, the clinical and the philosophical back to what proves to be the ultimately practical if man is to learn to manage his pain through more than chemical intervention.

The disciplined consciousness, which is comparable to the mystic's awareness, may be our next significant step in learning to manage pain creatively, so that we keep both our sensory awareness and the relief that comes with alpha dominance. If this process can be learned by people of one tradition, it can as well be mastered by practitioners of other cultures. For over fifty years I have been seeking to discipline my inner being. And although it may be a difficult thing to do, I am convinced that of all things in life it is the most worthwhile and least destructive. Not only can it relieve the disturbances that develop deep within but it can also provide the richest satisfactions deep within the self in the process.

Chapter 14

CREATIVITY AND PERSONAL GROWTH IN A MYSTIC

We hear much in our day about personality development. It is the primary datum for education, personality assessment, individual differences
and understanding the needs for psychotherapy. But we seldom have
much discussion of the total growth of the individual. Recently a large
book, Handbook of Developmental Psychology came to my study. In
nearly a thousand pages of two-column material exploring much of the
process involved in personal growth there is no reference to religion,
spirituality or human creativity. It would seem valid for our approach
to creativity to include the larger dimensions of personal growth, "in
stature, in wisdom and in favor with God and Man".

Personal growth is a wonderful thing to observe. On a built-in schedule governed by a minuscule gland at the base of the brain, the pituitary,
the baby becomes an infant and the infant a child. In good time the child

becomes the preadolescent and the adolescent the adult. Along the way the little gland makes contributions to some marvelous modifications of body structure and function. When all goes well physical growth follows a course well within the bounds of what we tend to call normal.

The growth is not always normal. A national magazine recently carried a story about a convention of dwarfs, the little people. In some way the pituitary did not do its job and the little people stopped growing well before they reached the size of their peers. Apparently normal in mental and emotional development they were faced with a whole variety of problems in a culture where most things were not their size. In the hotel where they met there was a problem with elevators. Many of the little people could not reach the button that indicated the floor to which they would travel. So the hotel provided batons that could be used to reach up to the desired button. In the dining room the chairs and tables were too high. The speakers needed boxes to stand on so that they could be seen over the podium. In a world not made for them, they were obliged to be the minority that adapted to what was acceptable for the majority.

Can you imagine what life would be like for the little people who tried to work in an office where all the equipment was made for larger people? Can you imagine what it would be like to supervise the growth of normal sized children where the problems of discipline would be multiplied by size differences and the inclinations of towering teenagers looking down on a little parent and saying, "make me" would be a strong temptation? Trying to live in a different sized world has complications.

Much the same problems can exist when the pituitary gland does not cease to produce the growth chemicals when it should. While it may be a financial asset for towering basketball players, it can create problems in day-to-day living. On a recent flight when the plane stopped to pick up passengers in a midwestern city the local professional basketball team came aboard. They bent low to come through the door and came down the aisle of the plane in stooped position and sat in seats designed for smaller people. Their knees were nearly at their chins and their discomfort throughout the flight was quite obvious. In a world made for middle sized people it is difficult to be too large or too small.

What is true of physical size is also true of social growth. I have spent considerable time working with groups of persons who reside in a federal penitentiary because their small sized behavior was unacceptable to the rest of society. Their thoughtless, vicious and undisciplined behavior was so reprehensible that society rejected their behavior and temporarily rejected them as well. Yet society also rejects those who are giants for social justice and for peace. Through history many Quakers have been jailed because they passed judgment on the warlike acts of their countries. George Fox and John Bunyan were not tolerated by the state. Martin Luther King and many of his colleagues in the civil rights movement were imprisoned not because they were criminals but rather because their human sensitivities were developed to the place where they could not tolerate injustice and cried out against it. Thus has it been for saints and prophets down through the ages. It seems to be hazardous to be too small or too big in social behavior.

Another area where growth is important is in the depth of spiritual adequacy. For instance, in monastic orders a novice would be assigned to a mature person who would serve as a spiritual guide. In other social and religious institutions this form of personal supervision of spiritual development was a well-defined form of education for centuries. Yet in recent years the role of the spiritual guide seems to have been replaced by other forms of teaching. If we are to appreciate and reestablish the role of the spiritual guide or counselor it is important for us to go back and examine the practices of the past, see what is valid in them, and then adapt them to the important tasks of encouraging spiritual growth in our day.

Again it is a matter of growth. Many shriveled souls seem afraid of the values that come with spiritual growth for they place too heavy a burden on life. Increased sensitivity causes increased distress in the presence of injustice and suffering. It seems that the emotional motivation for "meism" is related to this retreat into self-gratification in the presence of the afflictions that are a part of our society. In fact we see "meism" developed into a political philosophy when the needs of the helpless and the defenseless are ignored in order to give benefits to those who have political and financial power. Also this "meism" has a religious expression when people practice exclusions and hostility on the basis of arbitrarily established forms of judgment. "Believe as we believe or we will make life miserable for you, we will lie about you, we will vote against you, we will unjustly accuse you." The small attitude of the spiritual little people is actively expressed among us by single-issue groups, and self-proclaimed guardians of our morals by misnamed proponents of the "the moral majority".

When there is so much appeal and reward for littleness of spirit how can people in our day be encouraged to become spiritual giants, disciplined, devoted and devout? Perhaps we can operate on two fronts. There has been a growing interest in pastoral care in recent decades. After periods of uncertainty and interest in predominantly secular modes of intervention, an interest in the unique resources of the spiritual life seems to be developing. This may lead into a new interest in what I feel is the highest form of pastoral care, the role of the spiritual guide. This would naturally lead to a renewed interest in the forms of pastoral care used by the great spiritual guides of the past. Then perhaps we may be able to combine old methods and insights with newly developed tools to bring into focus the finest possibilities for spiritual growth.

Evelyn Underhill out of her wide experience as a guide for spiritual development and creative living says that the search begins with an all-pervading restlessness, a feeling of dissatisfaction with life as it has been lived. If at this time a person can be related to a spiritual guide the search may progress to a new focus for life's quest and finally a discovery of a sustaining relationship with the beyond self that is essentially within the self.

In this searching process the spiritual guide plays what appears to be a passive role. He does not manipulate or control the growing edge of the person guided. Rather it is a matter of being present, listening intently, sharing the search and as occasion warrants, asking the questions that keep the searcher on course. The pastoral counselor helps people adjust to life. The spiritual guide moves beyond a concern for adjustment to the achieving of a new level of perception of what life is about. It is a quest for the mature spirit, well beyond spiritual rompers or adolescent understandings. In that process the spiritual guide does not claim a superior knowledge for the insight that emerges from within is not evaluated in terms of more or less but rather in terms of achieving what is real and fulfilling at the deepest levels of living.

The spiritual guide is a companion on a quest, a patient companion willing to listen and explore free from either a special or hidden agenda. All the spiritual guide seeks is the freedom of his companion to grow toward his own potential. The spiritual guide has great confidence in the innate genius of the seeker. The spiritual guide trusts the inclination toward growth so implicitly that he would do nothing to interfere with that growth. In the "Cloud of Unknowing" we are told that true reality is "naught else but a true knowing and feeling of a man's self as he is".

Evelyn Underhill summarizes the goal of this quest in this manner. "We end, therefore, upon this conception of the psyche as the living force within us; a storehouse of ancient memories and animal tendencies, yet plastic, adaptable, ever pressing on and ever craving for more life and more love. Only the life of reality, the life rooted in communion with God, will ever satisfy that hungry spirit, or provide an adequate objective for its persistent onward push."

In this high form of pastoral care, the creative capacity to grow with another, a shared discipline seems to be the key that unlocks the door to new levels of growth. To relate to another human being with no desire to be dogmatic, dictatorial, manipulative nor authoritative calls for mutual trust and respect for the inner being of another.

That shows some of the essentials of the spiritual guide's approach to personal growth. First there is the restlessness, dissatisfaction with life as known. Then there is an in depth exploration of motivation, goals and resources. Then there is a sharing in complete honesty with someone who is completely nonjudgmental and totally responsive to the effort of the self to grow into greater adequacy. When the needs for growth appear to be attained the relationship is phased out so that the energy of life can be directed toward the achieving of goals instead of the search.

Another illustration comes out of a different form of restlessness and search. Often it seems that spiritual growth is a concomitant of personal crisis. The crisis supplies the energy of motivation for change, and the spiritual guide gently asks the questions that need to be asked to direct the energy seeking change toward the goal for which the change is sought. I first met Dr. Forsyth at a conference on consciousness at a retreat center in New England. We proved to be congenial in thought and practice. He was a physician whose practice has been deeply influenced by psychosomatic and psychogenic research. Because of the roles we shared in the conference we were brought closely together both in schedule and in shared perspectives. After the conference we went our separate ways and I did not hear from him for two years. Then he called me and said something had happened that he felt a desperate need to explore with someone a personal problem that was life engulfing. It had to be someone whose judgment he respected and whose personal integrity and ability to keep a confidence he trusted. I responded that I appreciated his trust and confidence and would do what I could to be worthy of it.

When we met my physician friend told me that he had a form of cancer that was difficult to treat and few survived its onslaught. He said that as a physician well schooled in psychosomatic and psychogenic medicine he understood the cause and effect factors operative. He knew that he was headed toward early death if he could not change the content of his consciousness. He felt it was a difficult task and almost impossible to do alone. But he thought I could help him do it. We soon agreed that his condition called for the best medical help that could be provided, but his concern was that treatment of the symptoms needed to be supplemented by treatment of the underlying personality factors that he felt were causative.

Time was an important factor so we spent many hours together in what amounted to a crash program of spiritual growth. He felt that his problems were essentially ethical, philosophical and ultimately theological. He had tried to manage life by outwitting the laws of cause and effect and he had apparently done well until his body began to act out his attitudes of ruthlessness and unrelenting manipulation of all of the other people in his life. In professional terms we might say that he was suffering from a severe personality disorder. He had successfully played fast and loose with the laws that usually govern life among humans. Now he was overwhelmed by the feeling that retribution was coming from within and was created by the chemical climate he had willfully created by his own attitudes and behavior. We admitted that he not only had a neoplastic condition that was difficult to treat but he also had one of the more difficult psychological conditions to cope with.

Like many people who live close to the seashore we spent many uninterrupted hours sailing the lake near his home. Instead of focusing on the mess he had made of his inner life and his human relations, we spent our time going back to see if we could understand how he had become the way he was. Then we spent many hours trying to help build a new perception of himself and others. We faced the task of creating a new person within him. Here we added to his fear of death and his self-hatred a new and more positive form of motivation. We worked to use the power and purpose and insight of religion to help achieve what might be called a personality transplant. It was far more than behavior modification, for it involved a new mental attitude toward himself and others, a new quality of emotional response to life, and a new spirit that could effectively direct his behavior in different channels.

The end result is not only a new person in spirit, but also a person who has survived the onslaught of his illness. He had good medical care to be sure. But with a form of the disease that is seldom effectively managed medically he has now had enough time without recurrence to feel that he is healed. More than that he feels that the important thing that has happened to him is the change in the inner climate where he felt the cause of his illness might be found. To be a spiritual guide on such a quest is not only a privilege but it is also a verification of the potential for growth even in the most threatening circumstances of body, mind and spirit.

To be sure, these accounts are so brief that they do not do justice to the long and sometimes painful process that is involved in spiritual growth. However, they do give some clues to the nature and purpose of this form of intervention.

Personal growth is a wonder filled experience. We see growth in body, mind and social adaptation as a constant and become concerned with the basic mechanisms of growth only when people are too small or too large in body, mind or social adaptation. The basic developing of the spiritual quality that can help to produce the fully developed human being may be overlooked. Yet creativity at its best always seems to depend on the spiritual quality that develops adequately. The equivalent of the pituitary gland of the spirit is neglected only at peril for all the rest of life. The growth can continue as long as life lasts, and we hope much longer.

Chapter 15

THE MYSTIC AS WORLD TRAVELER

During the last forty years I have spent a lot of time in travel and that travel has become an important part of my thinking and feeling. I have traveled to 36 countries in all of the major land areas of the world, North and South America, Europe, Africa and Asia as well as Australia and many of the islands of the sea. I have also been involved in reading the writings of people whose travels have been important in shaping their lives. Pierre Teilhard wrote about his adventures in travel as did Rockwell Kent about his various travels that stimulated his art. Even Thoreau who bragged that he traveled far in Concord wrote about his trips to the Maine woods and into Canada.

The mystical dimension of my being has been stimulated by my ventures into far places that breathed a sense of wonder and beauty that produced a lingering aura that would not leave, nor would I want it to go. Some part of many places has become a permanent part of my being that

I carry with me everywhere. In this chapter I will not try to deal with my impressions in an orderly or chronological manner but spontaneously as they flood into my consciousness. Will you go with me now into those experiences that have been triggered by places near and far?

My first real writing venture was a book on the mysticism of Henry David Thoreau. It was written in 1931 and I had spent many months saturating myself in the books of Thoreau as well as the books about him until I felt at home with him and his way of thinking. I felt that I would not complete my exploration of his being until I went to his favorite pond and breathed deeply of its flavor and its setting.

So I set out one morning to go to Walden and spent a day living in its environs. I arrived on a beautiful day in June and the part of the lakefront that had been made into a public park was crowded. I soon left the crowds behind me and wandered to the parts of the lakefront that had been more familiar to HDT. I was soon at the cairn that marked the spot of the cabin and soon found a shaded spot where I could meditate. As I sat under a tree I began to feel the mood that I thought appropriate. I traveled in thought back through the years and sought to relate to the soul I had grown to know so well through his books. In the isolation of that spot I lived again my thoughts as I wrote my little book about Thoreau. I have not been back to that spot though I have lived in New England much of my life. But that day and its thoughts and sights and feelings have been ever present with me through the many years since then. As with most mystical experiences they have become living events and an ever-accessible part of life. Thoreau's total resonance to the world of nature has been one of the basic perceptions that have enriched my life through nearly six decades.

I have always been fascinated by the cultures to our south and decided to take a trip to Peru and its unique civilizations as they showed up in ruins. Estelle and I visited friends in Lima and after a few days spent largely in museums we headed for Cuzco and its wonderful illustrations of old Inca artwork. One morning we arose early to take the daily train to Machu Pichu. After climbing mountains by a series of switch backs and arriving at the foot of a mountain we traveled up by a bus that mimicked the train except that it seemed to have a less secure hold upon the highway. When we alighted from the bus we caught our first view of the ancient jeweled city safely set in the recesses of the mountain. It took us some time to get used to breathing the rarefied air but soon we were heading up the trail that took us into the remains of the city of Machu Pichu. Every place we looked were examples of refined stone work for the masons of the time of its building were masters of their craft. Soon we were finished our explorations and found a quiet place where we could sit and contemplate the meaning of what we saw. People's inhumanity to people had left its destruction all about but behind the ruins was a story of creativity that caused incredible scenes of wonder. The eye of the mystic penetrated beyond the evidences of ruin to a quality of life that would have been impossible without some spark of the sacred that showed through. The return trip to Cuzco 80 miles away was filled with thoughts of wonder that have echoed through the intervening years.

The mystical awareness is not limited by bounds of national culture. I remember one day when I visited the temple of the thousand Buddhas. I was invited by the learned monk to study the faces of the thousand Buddhas until I found the one that was most like my own face. I took the assignment seriously and spent a good part of the day going up and down the long lines of statues that looked at me so peacefully and I began to find that something rather unusual was happening to me. Not only were the many statues beginning to look more like each other than they did at first but every person seemed to look strangely like every other person. It was as if the uniqueness of the individual was lost in the common humanity and through the power of the Buddha's vision the superficial differences that separate us were obliterated by an awareness of something greater that made us one. Since that day in Kyoto I have distrusted the first and quick view of another that may be deceptive and have tried to take that deeper look that characterized the perception of the mystic for there is something deeper in each one of us that may not be seen at first. Only the patient and discerning eye of the mystical consciousness may give us that perception that moves us beyond a type of blindness that is bound up with superficial things.

I have always been fascinated by Gothic cathedrals and the full structure of symbolic means that are bound up with their creation. I have made it a practice to light a candle and quietly meditate and contemplate while the candle burned itself out. I have found that some of my richest times of quiet exploration came as the result of such times of self-awareness.

Estelle and I had a chance to spend a couple of weeks at the Cathedral of Durham, living right within the cathedral compound. One of the earliest and most majestic of the great cathedrals of England, it has stood throughout nearly a thousand years. The quiet program of the cathedral school allowed plenty of time for exploring the high land upon which the building stood but also the castle that shared the uplands. We went to all the services to enjoy the wonder of its deep-throated organ. But most enjoyable of all was to enjoy the quietness of sunrise and sunset through the magnificent stained glass artwork of the windows that completely encircled the cathedral. The English cathedrals, which grew out of a wonderful period of English mysticism, were able to transform a worshiper into the mood of the builders. During two weeks when we saturated our souls in the symbolism and magnificence of Durham we added yet another dimension to our deep feeling of the mystical. When we left Durham and the cathedral and environs of the city we took much of it with us as a permanent part of our being. When shortly after, I was obliged to spend months in hospitalization I took along an artist's concept of the cathedral and it stimulated my spirit many times each day and I reentered the rarefied spirit of its personality and dwelt there in beauty and peace.

I spent many hours reading Henry Adam's Mt. San Michel and Chartres and when I lived in Paris saw Notre Dame every day. I saw a dozen other French gothic buildings and went to church many times in Beauvais. But I was transported in spirit at Mt. San Michel where every part of the experience conspired to add a spiritual perception to life. Seeing the Mont from miles away and approaching it slowly from the landside prepared me for its splendor. The long, winding walkway up the quaint approach helped create the perception that soon took over my consciousness. The cloister gave me a chance to sit and let my thoughts wander back through ages. When I was finally in the sanctuary I was well prepared mentally and spiritually to have an experience of wonder and spirituality. I lit my candle and settled my mind and thoughts for a couple of hours for ruminating. I thought my thoughts along with Henry Adams and shared his sensitivity of spirit along with my own heightened feelings as I let the place have its way with me. Of all the French churches this was unique in its location and its total absorption in its spiritual mission. I let it have its way with me until I felt completely transported and utterly possessed by its unique presence. When I finally pulled myself from its spell and reluctantly retraced my steps down from the heights I was a different person and was always sensitive to its power over me. Though I had taught in Benedictine seminaries and visited in the motherhouse in Rome no other place had exerted such a strong spiritual pull upon me. Though I would never return, I would never really leave that presence that gripped me spiritually and exerted its power over me.

The mystical presence can come from the things invested by the spirit of humans or it can come from the spirit resident in natural phenomena. One morning in McKinley national park Estelle and I arose early and caught a bus going out to the base of Mt. McKinley. On the way we were intrigued by the animal and bird life as the day was dawning. The crystal clear spring day was alive with the creatures that made their home in this protected habitat. Moose, caribou, foxes and smaller animals that abounded. Birds of many varieties and an occasional great white owl were very much alive along the way. We approached the view of the mountain suddenly so that it seemed to come upon us quickly. In its magnificence it was awesome. It stands taller than the tallest of the Himalayas because they start at several thousand feet while McKinley rises from the seacoast. On this day with its clearness the whole mountain stood out in all its grandeur. We viewed it from a promontory across a valley and were overwhelmed by its size as it towered majestically above us. It seemed a friendly mountain as it quietly possessed all it surveyed so that it could easily be seen from Fairbanks and Anchorage. It was easily surmounted by climbers many times over the last hundred years. Humankind has made a practice of glorifying high places as if they were somehow tinged with the mystical consciousness. Heights seem to take a hold of the consciousness in a unique way. The magnificence of that mountain that stood so quietly and powerfully before us that day, more than a dozen years ago, echoes in our awareness saying over and over again that our eyes are lifted up to that source of our being in a kinesthetic pull that speaks to all dimensions of our being.

Not all travel has been to places but some notable going has been toward people. Early in life I was aware of a man who could speak effectively to my depth of being. When in high school I turned on the radio every Sunday afternoon to hear him speak as he did with clarity and challenging intellect. When I went to seminary I studied preaching under his guidance. When he retired after a long and useful life, he moved into my community and I was able to spend hours with him exploring his thinking and feeling. These times were like a postgraduate course in communication where one could talk about the really important issues of life with a great master. He never lost the ability to speak of the great issues of life with relevance and discernment. Although I always felt that he was the great master he always treated me as an equal. When the time came for him to take his place among the immortals I was surprised one day to receive a communication from England asking me if

I would write his biography for an Encyclopedia. This I was honored to do and felt privileged as I spent a summer rereading all of his books that I fortunately had in my library. I felt that this was an opportunity to re-immerse myself in the works of his mind and spirit. The richness of the spirit along with the acuteness of his mind made him a great resource for understanding the richness of the Christian tradition as his intellect digested it. Although he did not talk much about mysticism he breathed an understanding of how it could transform life with purpose and insight. While I had so much respect for his uniqueness I never tried to copy his preaching. His way of speaking became a model that I was always aware of and owed much to his example. I am sure you knew that I spoke of Harry Emerson Fosdick. It was an honor to know him.

I had an unusual chance to live in Greece for six months. During that time I did some lecturing in American institutions at the Greek Orthodox Seminary in Athens and lots of coming and going in historic places. Years before I had studied classical and New Testament Greek, and had a little working knowledge of the language though not too much familiarity with contemporary Greek. I was deeply interested in the early manifestations of mysticism and the practices of the mystery religions such as those at Eleusis. I traveled out there during the daytime and explored around the temple but understood that the most provocative experiences were had on moonlit nights. One night when the moon was full I went out there and made my way to the ruins of the temple, roamed around for a while and then sought out a place that looked comfortable and promising. I tried to bring my mind to a contemplative mood and thought back over what I had learned of the Eleusinian mysteries, their thoughts of death and resurrection and the promises of those initiated into the mysteries. This was the practice of mysticism during the time before Plato and his followers. The moonlight gave an eerie glow to old marble and I prepared myself for an unusual happening that might occur. Nothing unusual took place and although my inner being was stimulated to enjoy lovely thoughts nothing that I perceived as unusually mystical took place. But after hours of trying for a special awareness there was only the feeling of a benevolent presence permeating my being. I had the feeling that my uninitiated status precluded me from the more spectacular manifestations or perhaps they were only imaginary among those who were committed to the religious. At any rate I spent a most pleasant night in a wonderful spot and had the feeling that it was a special place. The mystical awareness was present in my being but it was no more nor less than it was in other sacred spots where I had spent time reaching out to be aware.

Places of magnetic power are supposed to explain those spots on the earth's surface that had special qualities akin to energy. These could be found at Avebury and Stonehenge and other places where ancients located their places of worship. Also these spots of psychic energy were found at Chartres and other sacred spots. There are many in England, Brittany and France. While visiting Ireland I checked out some sacred spots around the countryside. Druids were said to worship in scattered places in Ireland. Near where we were visiting in Raphoe, not far from Malin Head at the northern tip of the country, there was a place with large perpendicular columns of stones. There was nothing to mark the place as special or unusual. The field was fenced and within were hundreds of sheep. I climbed the fence and sat on top the fence post. I tried to imagine these same fields four or five thousand years ago with the people who were the inhabitants then. With special astronomical knowledge and strong religious sensitivity they expended great energy and skills to prepare and maintain their places of worship. Had they been wiped out or amalgamated by the process of time and change? There has been much speculation concerning these people and what happened to them. Perhaps we are the descendants of these people. But there is one thing that is quite sure and that is that they were well endowed with a strong mystical sense that motivated their thinking and actions. Maybe some anthropologist will turn up some evidence that will give us some knowledge of our forebears. Our search for roots may make us more aware of those early qualities of mind and spirit that make us akin to long lines of ancestors who share a mystical heritage.

As a child my father took me to Serpent Mound and Fort Ancient. I had been back to the puzzling monuments several times on geology explorations in Ohio and other parts of the country and have found that mysteries abound here as well as in Europe. People of intellect shared these places for these many centuries. They wanted to relate themselves to moon and stars and were moved by the spirit with them to seek meaning in those things that they did not fully understand. The universal symbol of the snake that modern psychologists find is present in the dream life of every culture, even the Eskimos who have no experience with serpents. Late studies indicate that roots of our ancestors may go back at least fifteen thousand years and have shared and lost cultures that have come and gone with the years. We may have lost more sophisticated cultures that had climbed farther to the ladder of mystical sensitiveness. Rolling Thunder, the Indian medicine man, speaks of wisdom they do not share with the White Man for they do not trust this last culture to properly protect the knowledge they have acquired through long and patient exploration. When it comes to learning the ways of the mystic sensitiveness we perhaps have far to go. When my father said he hoped I would learn many of the secrets of the early inhabitants of this land who have long gone I wonder if we are prepared to handle the wonders they knew and treasured. Only as we are able to learn and practice new levels of the mystic consciousness will that be possible. We have yet much work to be done.

The Uniting Church in Australia was having a celebration of the act of coming together and decided to recognize it by a special event. They planned to have a lectureship on pastoral work and they chose me to give the lectures. Instead of them coming together in one place they chose to have me travel to the local districts. So I spoke one hundred and twenty times in thirty days over a travel route of seven thousand five hundred miles. But the place that appealed to me most was the "out back". I visited a parish that covered over a thousand miles that was covered by two Sundays and one midweek service. It was beyond the Flinders Range of mountains. I shared one Sunday of that circuit but it was enough to give me a taste of its vast expanse. One would drive a hundred miles without seeing a human habitation and for companionship would have to be content with kangaroos and emus and lots of smaller animals. When at evening we would gather at a home we would glory in human fellowship. I found that these people had a whole different sense of companionship. Where in a city there might be two thousand people to a square mile, in the "out back" there might be one person to a thousand square miles. That could affect the social sense in a very real way. A person would have to depend on the self that had been created by inner processes to sustain life at its depth. I had to get on with the tight schedule prepared for me but I would have enjoyed stopping off to spend a few months in such a completely new atmosphere and see what it would produce. To achieve the mystics consciousness there has to be a winnowing away of the trivial foci of the mind. I am inclined to think the vastness of space and the freedom from distraction would serve a useful purpose. I detected a different perspective on life when the human quality was spread thin and the truer meaning of life had a chance to shine through.

After the strenuous efforts of the lecture trip in Australia, Estelle and I went up to Cairns in Queensland for a week's relaxation and some chance to see new things. We headed for the wonders of the Great Barrier Reef. We could encompass but a small part of it but what we saw was staggering in its beauty and infinite variety of sea life. We traveled far out upon the reef and spent many hours looking at the myriad forms of sea life and color that abounded there. We thought of the power reflected in such evidences of creative power. I was filled with a sense of limited knowledge and understanding as we stood before the magnificence of these created wonders that were here for untold ages going through the patient process of being and becoming and would continue to become new and wonderful creatures through infinite time. Then I thought of human depredations that might commit the ultimate act of sacrilege as their destructiveness might bring this wonderful creation to a staggering halt and end the processes of ever new and wonderful life forms. In the struggle of God's creative forces against human destructiveness we are coming close to a final decision. The mystical consciousness can let the creativeness of God show through within and without only if the processes of destruction are held in check. Everywhere I go two major forms of human fear are held before our eyes as if we have but to define which we will choose. The mystic's choice of the creative power of God is clear. When we stand before the splendor of God at work in the patient ways of time and history we see the alternative ever more clearly. The Great Barrier Reef is a parable that speaks to us of creation and its wonder and beauty. Can we hear and heed before it is too late?

I visited the ruins of the palace of King Minos on the northern coast of Crete. No one was about and the only other sign of life was a salamander about six inches long. It was as if we alone had inherited these premises from the accumulation of the ages. What a symbol that could be as we look at the possibilities of the future. Will we share it with lizards or will they have it all to themselves? Will we make room for a higher consciousness or will we blunder into oblivion? That seems to be the question that now faces us.

Chapter 16

THE CATHOLIC CHURCH AND MYSTICISM

The Catholic Church has produced some of the great mystical spirits of Christendom and yet the Catholic Church as an institution has always been suspicious of mystics and burned many of them at the stake during the time of persecution in the Inquisition. In college I made a special study of Giordano Bruno to see if I could understand the issues that lead to his cruel execution and the sweeping of his ashes into the Arno.

Yet the Catholic Church played a major role in holding European civilization together for centuries after the fall of the Roman Empire. How could the church play such a contradictory role in society? It would take more space and time than we have at our disposal to go into the many forces of ecclesiastical history that played a part in the process. Before the church split in the great schism the Eastern part had a strong mystical flavor as it has continued to favor the nonmaterialistic concept. During the six months that I was intimately identified with that part of

Christendom I had a chance to feel the differences between East and West. The attitude of mind was different even down to the slightest detail. My lectures in Greece concerning the history and practice of the Church in the United States brought forth all manner of questions that showed a complete lack of comprehension of the freedom of thought and actions that existed and separated the major branches of Christendom. The mood of the Eastern Church showed a historic development that was essentially different from the Western Church. It was an accident of time and circumstance but it was so deep that it could not be worked through in the councils of East and West. The split was such that it has never been bridged and the West's antagonism to the mystic flavor of the East combined the fear of the free moving spirit of the uncontrolled authority of the East keeps the breach intact through a thousand years.

This basic question about the Catholic Church that had been unanswered in my mind was tackled when I made my way to seminary. I chose as the major project of my senior thesis the Summa Theologica of St. Thomas Aquinas. I went through the twenty volumes of his life's work with plenty of skipping of those things bound up with his time and mental frame of his age. The logic and prior assumptions of his work were a revelation to me and I was deeply effected by the power of his logic granted his assumptions. It was a tight work of scholarship that held true to Aristotelian methods and as long as it was approached with Aristotle's assumptions it was valid, but when it encountered newer ways of thinking it showed its inadequacies. But having the Summa to refer back to always made it possible to understand the medieval scholars' thought processes and their inadequacies. Little did I know that I would soon have a chance to test out my thinking concerning the Catholic Church from the inside.

During the final stages of the War in Europe they needed someone to be actively engaged in managing the distribution of emergency relief supplies in Italy. I was chosen for that assignment and on a brief notice I found myself attached to the Vatican staff to supervise the correlation of

172

the distribution of material for relief of the destitute civilian population. I was immediately given stature and authority among Vatican personnel. Our state department, which under normal conditions was allowed to work only with other official governmental agencies, was allowed to use its regular church channels for distribution of supplies. This worked out well for the church had clinics in almost every village in the country already at work and they provided the agency for transport and distribution of medical supplies and other forms of relief such as blankets, food and clothing. We were not so much concerned with who received the credit for the prevailing conditions dictated that we use what was available without too much evaluation. For a brief period of time I was given the best cooperation imaginable.

The conditions made it possible to have a quality of ecumenical action that was virtually impossible at other times. There was a tradition of non-cooperation in joint services for the Catholics always wanted their services to have a prior claim over any other. One of our planes was downed and in the ensuing fire all material and personnel were reduced to unidentifiable remains. It was found that there were Protestant, Catholic and Eastern Orthodox members of the crew and it was decided by our commanding officer that we were to have a joint service. The plan for the service was explained to all involved and the Catholic clergy demurred but when it was explained that they could cooperate in an ecumenical service or be excused entirely from the moment of memorial they revised their thinking and shared in the joint service with the other clergy. It was as far as we knew the only service of all three branches of the Christian church meeting together at one and the same time and place.

During the time that I had that assignment there were periods of leisure between the arrival and shipping of relief supplies. I spent many hours wandering around the Vatican library and exploring the archives as a privileged insider. I realized the opportunity afforded me for research and study and I always had at hand the staff secretary who translated for me and answered my many questions. I had studied New Testament Greek as well as classical Greek, Latin, French, German and Spanish besides my basic English so I had enough language facility to help in my explorations and to check up on the facility of my translator. William Morris III had done some research in the Vatican library on groups of iconoclasts who had been lost track of or escaped through historical references in the Vatican library. This was also true of the Cathori who were active in Southern France and Northern Italy after the time of St. Francis. I completed my assignment with the government before I had done all of my own private exploration in the library and archives. I had to return to explore further with some time at the Waldensien Seminary where they were most helpful. Also Fr. Beckes the director of the Benedictine House which is the center for the worldwide order gave of his time and wisdom during a two week sojourn in Rome. All of this convinced me that there is a lot of obscured history that is interesting and would profitably be brought to light. It seemed that much of this conflict was motivated by a desire to bring under rigid ecclesiastical control those portions of the church that followed the mystical impulse, for if the church were ever to become powerful it must be under the absolute control of an uncompromising authority.

For hundreds of years the church at Rome tried to bring under its control the mystical impulse that burst forth after the time of St. Francis. In a cruel and relentless crusade most of the flower children of that period were exterminated. Zoe Oldenberg in a series of books recounted the story of that period and indicated how many of those of the mystical persuasion went underground in Switzerland, France and England. Much of the history of the time is lost because the secret orders such as the Masons kept it from common knowledge. Some of the refugees from the crusades retreated into the recesses of the Alps and remained there for centuries. It was necessary for them to remain in their places of retreat and seclusion well through the times of the Inquisition. The Waldensians, Albigensians and other remnants of the long persecution of the mystical group within remained in seclusion until this last century when the active persecution ended and the new freedom within society became guaranteed. The library of the Waldensian Seminary in Rome provided some of the missing links between the original impulse after the time of St. Francis and the modern era.

My wife and I made a couple of trips to Sion in the upper Rhone valley of Switzerland where the mystics of the twelfth and thirteen centuries established a vigorous pocket of resistance but apart from a primitive old organ in the church on the hill there seemed to be little left from that period of history. In spite of the strenuous effort of the Church in Rome to blot out the uncontrolled efforts of the mystical impulse that persisted in many and devious ways there is little doubt that the Protestant Reformation was bound up with the original mystical impulse within the Church. William Morris found many connections between the many revolts within the Church, which only live in the records of their defeat as recorded in the Vatican library. But the movement was kept alive in such movements as the Hussites and live in their powerful choral music which led them in their revolts a hundred years before Luther and provided the ties with the troubadours who were agents of the underground movement of the church and were early fomenters of the free life that became the reformation later on. But there is no doubt that the mysticism that was so strong in the Eastern church persisted after the schism and the vigorous efforts to eradicate it were futile even though much blood and turmoil was spent in the effort.

Within the Church and even during the crusade against the mystics there was an active movement within the monastic orders to pursue the mood of mysticism. Even when the inquisition was at its most ruthless in its persecutions the devout souls were following their mystic bent. In the Cloud of Unknowing the unidentified author indicated that a mystical presence seems to pervade his world with a perception that is more than mere reality but is a something beyond that makes all else a revelation of exquisite meaning. Jacob Boehme said that in moments of awareness he saw into the essence of things and beings. These Rhineland mystics appeared to have an open perception that illuminated all there was with a deeper meaning. Meister Eckhart developed the inner being when the usual boundaries were eliminated and the spiritual essence was guaranteed by complete giving of the self to those cosmic dimensions measured by nonmaterial being. Jan van Ruysabroech, another of the Rhineland Mystics, saw his relationship as 'above reason and beyond reason' so that it had to be acceptable within the church. They all shared a common devotion to a spiritual relationship greater than any human authority. Also St. Theresa and St. John of the Cross shared the same mood of mysticism although they came from a differing time and tradition. There was something in the church that kept producing an inner authority that was paramount. As long as that impulse within the church was quiescent and caused no revolt against the authority of the church it was tolerated but when it caused open questioning of authority as with the Cathori all of the power of the church plus such civil authority as could be assayed against it was brought to bear to eliminate the opposition.

Shortly after I retired I received a letter from my friend who was the academic dean of St. John's Benedictine seminary in Minnesota. He invited me to meet with the faculty in the lounge in Collegeville. At the time and place prearranged we gathered and I surmised what might be happening when I saw a number of my books displayed on the coffee table. For an hour or so we talked about books and my purposes in writing them. Then my friend the dean said that he would like to say something. He said that in the modern church a growing emphasis was on pastoral care and it was well known that the Catholic church had dealt with pastoral theology through dogma and ritual primarily. Now that it was established that the people were the church there had to be a modification of emphasis. The Catholic church had not emphasized pastoral care in the past and so had not developed specialists in that field. So they had studied those who were teaching and practicing pastoral care in the present. They found that the leaders in that discipline were seminary oriented with one exception. Then looking at me he said I was the exception and because they wanted to be parish oriented they would like to invite me to join their faculty. After a few appropriate comments and invitation to continue the discussion with sharper focus we adjourned for more talk with the dean and heads of the related departments. While I had been invited by several other seminaries of my own denomination and others of the Protestant tradition in this country and abroad I had never been approached in quite the same manner and especially in the Catholic family of seminaries. I thanked Fr. Kieren Nolan for the gracious invitation and assured him that I would give it careful consideration and would give my answer within a few days. In time I agreed to be an occasional lecturer and to be willing to teach in their summer school but that because of my state in life and my previous commitments I would not be able to accept his kind offer though at a different time in my life I would have jumped at the opportunity. From time to time I have enjoyed the privilege of sharing fraternal relationship with my colleagues of the Catholic church in this country and abroad and am glad to say that the climate that they created is most commendable. I will say nothing about the great step backward that has been taken by the present occupant of the chair of St. Peters. As a frequent lecturer at Catholic University I sense the restlessness in the academic community caused by the present circumstance.

I was at one time closely related to the Winnegrun Foundation, which for many years supported the work and research of Pierre Teilhard de Chardin the Jesuit paleontologist. So I was aware of the behind the scenes struggle to have his scientific work accepted and approved by the Catholic Church. While he was true to the teachings of the Church none of his writings were given the stamp of approval by the Church until after his death. He formulated a structure of relationship that made it possible through the use of philosophical mystical concepts to find the deeper meanings of scientific truth.

Pierre Teilhard brought together long practiced strands of mystical thought and added to them immeasurably. His mother considered

Voltaire as one of her forebears while on his father's side he owned the scientific mystic Pascal. As a youth he was led toward both the Church and the world of scientific research. In his early years he was a teacher of physics in Egypt and established his interest and perpetuation as a careful and accurate observer of phenomenon related to science. He was also deeply interested in the meaning of his observations. His mind was always working to establish patterns and structure in what he observed. He became deeply interested in the evolution of all life but especially of man. He spent about a third of his life doing pioneer work in the back country of China looking carefully at the evolutionary processes as he observed them. He gained a well-deserved reputation among his scientific colleagues for his innovative work in paleontology but made no effort among them to develop his philosophical ideas on religious thinking. He kept careful notebooks and journals and with time put them into proper condition for publication if the Church ever lifted its ban on their release. That never happened during his lifetime but his works were eagerly awaited upon his death and it was then that his influence as a churchman was added to his already recognized stature as a scientific thinker. He had developed a plan of development that not only made the discoveries of science acceptable but also gave a picture of the future that was acceptable to those who felt that science should not lead humanity in to a dead end. He saw purpose and meaning in every step of the process and gave to it the power and wisdom and direction of Divine process.

In a world that was whirling toward its own destruction by ignorant men who abused the power that was placed in their hands the writings of Pierre Teilhard gave an alternative that thinking persons would respect and follow. In schools of higher learning his writings and thought were carefully considered and its insights pondered. In a world that was preoccupied with war and destruction his way gave new hope and purpose to history. During these years I was traveling to Catholic schools and disciplined orders. I well remember leading the retreat at a Day of

Rededication for Sisters of the Order of St. Joseph of Corondelet. About five hundred members of the Order from all over the country came together for this day of meditation and prayer and renewing of friendship ties. It was a memorable day with noble sentiments expressed by these women who went back to the lonely assignments one by one but renewed in their purpose. I tried to give them some of Pierre Teilhard's view of the future toward which they could all work for he brought together the best of the world of science and the hope of the world of the future as God in his purpose would reveal it in the future yet to be revealed. The head of the program committee gave me as I left for the plane a little book on the Beatitudes, which I read on the plane returning home. It was a perfect ending for a day with the mystical visions of a Catholic mystic who saw the world with the wonder of a religious mystic who spoke out of the long tradition of being in the world but not of it. The vision is fragile and hard to hold onto with mortal hands but it is the life of the spirit that endures in spite of the persecution and all manner of tribulation. It will still be there when all else is done away.

The first time I visited the Sistine Chapel I was alone and there were no tourists around. The atmosphere was desolate for the war had oppressed the world with its destructiveness but at least there was no one to tell me I could not lie on the floor for that is the only way to really study the ceiling with out getting a neck ache. For a while I was uninterrupted but then I heard others walking around and thought it was time to change my position. Many times since I have looked at reproductions of that magnificent piece of art and always see it with awe and wonder. This Michael Angelo work is without doubt one of the most magnificent representations of creation that was done in his time or any time. The Catholic Church has been hospitable to such works of mystical imagination. Not like the Protestant Church in Oklahoma where the figure of Adam and God was made the subject of a move to cover it as pornographic, the Catholic Church has mixed tolerance and judgment to suit its own taste. My recent visit to the Sistine Chapel was quite different.

179

The place was so crowded with people and there was such a buzzing of talking that the sacred beauty of the place was called into question. In the beautiful chapel it shows its effort to combine two forces that are at best incompatible and at worst committed to deadly struggle. Yet there is enough strength in the Church to survive the incessant conflict between the external and materialistic nature of the organization and the inner spirit of its life that is constantly breaking forth in true and pure mystical expression.

The effort to bridge this chasm is a condition that has plagued the Church and probably will continue to plague the world of careful scholarship. I received a letter from the head of the department of psychiatry at Harvard Medical School a while ago asking me to write a letter recommending a Jesuit scholar to become a member of the faculty of the school. The scholar was admirably qualified, well trained as a physician and also well trained in philosophy. The head of the department indicated that he feared the limited perspective of the other members of the department would assert itself and would reject the candidate on the basis of their prejudice rather than accept him because of his qualifications and their needs. I worked long and hard over that letter because I knew it would be easy to have my point of view rejected. I went briefly into the history of psychiatry and dealt with the much longer perspective that might be considered from the point of view of other disciplines. These other disciplines might have many valuable insights obscured by the prejudices that have accrued during the years. There seems no better time than the present to engage in the process of winnowing the wheat from the chaff and probably no better person would exist than one carefully trained in both of the disciplines involved. After careful consideration and evaluating all of the circumstances involved it was decided to invite him to become a member of the faculty. He subsequently has been selected by Scientific American to be their regular consultant in the cumulative supplement of psychiatry, which is the method the Journal uses to keep their readers abreast of the important developments in the field of their specialization.

There have been many struggles along the way that have obscured the contributions of the Church to the importance of mysticism. Those who understand it have no trouble making a proper place for it, recognizing that mysticism is yet another level of perception and that there is always a place for that kind of thinking. It will probably be a long time before the mystical mood will be entirely welcomed in the historical adjustment that will have to take place before East and West are at home with each other and the spiritual soul of the Church is at home with the materialistic body which is always asserting its influence.

We can all be thankful for the moving spirits within the Catholic Church who preserved its life in times of trial and inner conflict. We may shudder at the vain pomp and glitter, which shows in much of its life as we glory in the heroic souls from Bruno to Teilhard. Their integrity and singleness of purpose give meaning to the empty trappings. They witness to the life of the mystic who gains life from the action and reactions of history and always proves that a deeper life is asserting itself. The mysticism will always be the substance and the institution the framework that supports its life. The mystical spirit will surely outlive the materialistic framework that surrounds it. In spite of itself the Church has kept alive and nourished the spirit that comes to life within its many faceted life and thus mysticism will live on and flourish.

Chapter 17

PRAYER AS THE MYSTIC USES IT

As long as humans are questing for the meaning of the consciousness of life they will continue the process of prayer in one form or another. Sometimes in the very denial of prayer they are affirming its effect upon their minds. The knowledge that they can move beyond the casual manipulation of their own minds is an admission that there is a realm beyond the easy reach of every day consciousness that is beyond their understanding. There needs to be some way of engaging this extension of consciousness they can make. From the beginning of time human spirits have felt that something within themselves could communicate with this extension of themselves. Some have formalized this process to the place where they gave it a name and a more formal method of communication. Others admitted their lack of understanding of what was beyond them but they sought to show resonance for it by paying attention to the fuller possibilities of this communication in the constant process of meditation and contemplation. Basically there are only two types of response that can be made. There is the way of the reductionist or the unbeliever and the negative form of assumption immediately cuts off the possibility of any progress at that point. The other alternative is the one that the mystic employs and that is based on the assumption of an unknown possibility based on the infinite mathematics of cerebral potential. This takes the "maybe, yes" approach.

The negative approach serves the emotional needs of the timid and unadventurous. It pulls the function of the imagination down tight around the mind so that it dares not venture beyond the rigid control that practical understanding permits.

In this approach, there is no room for the exploring mind to dare its ventures into the experimental realm of thought. The chains of materialism bind it tight as if there were nothing beyond the limits of the material to explore. It is so afraid of the soaring imagination that it fears the consequences of the unbridled delving into the consciousness and its ability to discover areas of meaning beyond the bounds laid down by reductionism. It would deny to the mind those explorations that would push out the boundaries of awareness beyond those limits set by the cautious and denying attitudes of mind that govern the reductionist. Whole realms of human experience are declared off limits and they seek their satisfaction in the limits and failures of human kind. They appear to fear the full realization of their possibilities as human beings and are content to go through life hobbled by the ideas that come from their doubts and fears.

The mystic uses prayer with a full range of possibilities. It is not a use of meaningless rote, which cramps the mind into a limited form of self-indulgence, but rather seeks the meaning that is beyond form and repetition. It sees prayer as the most audacious stretching of the mind possible as the person uses the mental capacity to move beyond the limits of prayer set by tradition and common practice. It becomes a practice of the mind seeking to get beyond itself in the exploration of the boundaries that have traditionally been set for it. Traditional prayer is used as a device of a limited being for small purposes by a creature that sees beyond the boundaries of mind to suit a view of a small cosmos with a personal Deity exerting control from a limited cosmic stance. It is a small concept of humanity acted out on a stage that is bounded by a small imagination.

That kind of prayer is made to order for the limited mind but it has no place in the mind of the true mystic. I was brought up in the tradition that used prayer as an extension of the preacher's opportunity to mold the minds of the congregation. I used the chance to listen to see what the dynamics were and also to consider some crass measurements. By my watch one such prayer lasted twenty minutes and was a synopsis of human history pointing out how the Cosmic Being had run the affairs of humanity through the ages.

The arrogance of little people who felt comfortable with a little God was too evident. This is opposite the stance of the mystic, who stands humbly before the unknown and seeks to find out what may be revealed. The seeking mind and the sought revelation are in a constant dialogue of spirit and as the seeking mind proves to be worthy it is revealed to the seeking mind and heart. The mystic's prayer is not the presumptive storming at the gates of heaven but rather is the quiet seeking for the truth that may be shown to those who are ready to receive it. As age succeeds age the universe becomes more wonderful to behold and the less likely is it that the majesty and order of the universe is apt to be thrown out of kilter by the importunings of individuals who reside in a third rate universe in one of the billions of galaxies of which creation is a part. We have to grow up to the place where we see creation as it is and our place in it as it is. We must begin to live as if we have heard about the Copernican revolution and have taken it seriously. A lot has happened since Galileo looked through his tube on that January night in the year 1600 and we cannot act as if it did not happen. We cannot continually refuse to recognize the dimensions of the creation our scientists have revealed to us in the last four hundred years because it is here to stay.

We are obliged to redefine our idea of prayer to fit our universe. We must readjust our concepts so that the last four thousand years conform to the cosmic pattern rather than try to make the history of the world conform to the perception of a relatively small group of desert roaming nomads. Each age must define its concept of ultimate reality so that it takes account of the dimensions it uses in dealing with its own idea of boundaries. It cannot use the dimensions of one age in measuring the boundaries of another. It confuses the mind if it measures light years by cubits. It confounds the mind when it tries to limit the measurements of our age by those of a time of mathematics limited by ten fingers. And social standards cannot be limited to a concept of justice that confuses the divine right of kings with the divine right of any human being. Our theology and our cosmology must coincide or we work at cross-purposes. Our idea of ultimate reality and our concept of the universe must not argue with each other. Our concept of prayer and astrophysics must be at peace with each other. We cannot conceive of prayer at the end of this century as we did at the beginning of it. The mystic has the clear advantage in being comfortable at either end of the century because his idea of reality is free floating and is not bound by a rigid idea of either cosmology or theology.

Then prayer is not aimed at the cosmic other as much as it is an exploration for resonance within the bounds of consciousness. Once having said that, we know that we are more honest with ourselves in a much more lonely universe. We cannot use the gift of consciousness to play games with products of consciousness that we create. The super-structure of our imagined spiritual society then appears to be without foundation for we have created the society to keep ourselves company. But we need not be desolated by the feeling of cosmic loneliness for we can find the other dimension of ourselves in the richer life of our consciousness which we had little imagined before this century with its more careful study of the superconscious. At the beginning of this century our researches into the wonders of the mind and consciousness were mostly related to the subconscious. Dr. Freud started a revolution centered in the exploration of the preconscious and the unconscious and their impact on the subconscious. We took time to digest the past before we understood the riches of the present and the future.

The studies of the brain and its physiology that have taken place in recent decades have illuminated what we know about the brain in two directions. We not only know much more about the intricacies of its functioning but we also know that we cannot know effectively the hundred of billions of interactions that can take place within the space of a second. Our supercomputers can do wonderful things but their limitations are finite. The mathematical calculations that are involved in raising ten thousand million to the twenty-five thousandth power is more than any machine can begin to calculate. The implication of this is that we cannot know the functioning of our own brain; therefore we are always working with assumptions and approximations. We move beyond the basic requirements of the scientific method very quickly. The higher reaches of science hasten our mental limits and we are quickly at the point where we are obliged to make our assumptions much like the mystic makes his leap of faith. We go as far as we can go with the aid of science and logic but we soon arrive at the place where we must move into the unknown. Then we decide how we shall proceed by other forms of value judgment.

The mystic has a certain advantage at this point for he has learned to be comfortable with leaps of faith. Instead of the mind that is bound by dogmas and prejudices the mystic is free to move toward ideas large enough to accept the best that is known and at the same time imagine the best that is possible to project. The mind that is limited by the assumptions of a creed or a dogma is never free to make the larger assumptions of the image-creating spirit. Nor is it ever able to free itself from the limitations any inherited structure subtly demands of adherents. A person

186

may spend much of life trying to outgrow the limitations of an inherited perspective and allow the mystical awareness to exert itself. Instead of depending on some institution or other person to reach out in exploration the mystic is free to approach the unseen with the most audacious projections of consciousness. Then the process of prayer is free to explore the depths of consciousness without compromise or hesitation. Prayer then becomes the true realm of the spirit uncluttered by those attitudes that come with any predisposing of consciousness by prejudice, fear or theological misgiving. This guarantees that the mystic at prayer is able to exercise true spiritual freedom impossible to achieve when mind and spirit are trammeled by tradition and bound by verbal restraint.

The mystic uses the freedom that is implicit in the nature of the mystic's life view. Given by nature to prayer and contemplation he is always moving out upon uncharted areas of mental exploration. Without being hobbled by other people's ideas of how the mind should limit its explorations it is possible for the mystic to move out into new and fruitful areas of exploration. Because of the exploration of the possibilities of meditation and contemplation the mystic is free of preconceived ideas and false boundaries nothing seems to surpass the mystic at prayer. The prayer of the mystic is a special type of thinking. It is not the thinking that closes in upon the self but is rather concerned with freeing the self from any of the limitations that would be impinging on that self. This type of prayer seeks to move beyond verbal symbols so that it is freed from normal restraints that come with words or word thoughts. But rather than being a free-floating consciousness it is a direction of thought with a general rather than a specific direction. It opens all of consciousness to the cosmic process and the cosmic awareness without trying to control the thinking process. In this way it increases the mystical awareness without preempting the content of consciousness. In this way it provides a way for responsiveness to the cosmic spirit without cluttering of the thought processes by an overactive ego.

Mysticism is the higher development of the inner kingdom in which the individual consciousness and the cosmic consciousness are in such intimate correspondence that the boundaries between self and beyond self appear to become irrelevant and the power and purpose of God are directly manifest. The mystical awareness is an achievement of the discipline of consciousness so that it is able to fulfill the higher possibilities of what psychologists call the superconscious state.

Mysticism is always a personal achievement. While it is possible for a group of likeminded people to create the external atmosphere that may foster the mystical consciousness, the ultimate experience is always intensely personal. As Lawrence LeShan points out in his book Alternate Realities, human consciousness has a dimension that he calls the "inventive-creative capacity". At this point the intensely focused and carefully disciplined consciousness moves into an organization and direction of energy that produces something entirely new and participates in creation as a part of it. What is referred to as prayer in its more refined and disciplined form creates the conditions that make the mystical consciousness with its special powers a possibility.

In other fields of human endeavor the mystical experience takes different form. Marc Chagall showed it in his mastery of color, as El Greco reflected it in his genius with form. Thoreau achieved a mystical relationship with nature just as Bach and Franck did with music. It seems to be a process where the inventive-creative capacity infused the raw material of life with a new and richer meaning. The experience Jacob Needleman speaks of as a sense of the cosmos brings subtle change to what existed before. In a sense the impersonal is personalized and in the process becomes something new.

Lord Adrian and his colleague Sir John Eccles try to explain the neurophysical process involved in this inventive and creative function of the human mind. They face a mystery that occurs when the physical equipment of the brain is transcended by something mental through which the merely physical becomes something more. Here may be the mystery that lies at the center of a new theology and it may be that the uniqueness of Jesus was that he discovered the possibility for this transcendent nature of consciousness and sought to reveal it to other humans.

Chapter 18

HOW THE MYSTIC LOOKS AT DEATH

Very often there are factors that exert a major control of life for which the individual seems to have no influence. Such was the case with me and the matter of death. It has played a most significant part in my life and I would not have chosen any of it if I had been able to choose for myself. In any effort to understand the forces that shaped my life I think I would have to take a long and candid look at what death has done to shape my destiny. I know people that have had no first hand knowledge of death. In fact for many persons growing up in the contemporary world they have reached mature years without having to face any death in their immediate circle of family or friends. Certainly this would have an important bearing upon life itself. It would be one of the significant experiences that would have a bearing on my own life.

Probably I am known to most people as an interpreter of the experience of death and as one who has been able to look at it unflinchingly and thus be able to help the grief stricken to confront their overpowering emotions and learn to deal with them creatively. In childhood I was able to know what it was like to be held in the parenthesis of death for my older brother and younger sister both died before I was more than eight years of age. As an adult my wife and I have known death as a close personal experience as both of our sons have died untimely deaths. There was time when I would have thought grief would be the last subject upon which I would have shown any special knowledge, yet I have written ten books on the subject, most of them on request. When being introduced to the audience at Columbia University it was said that I knew more about the subject than any one alive. That was not a very enviable thing to say but the professor who said it must have believed it was true. Thousands of addresses later I can say that I encountered more people's deep feelings than I had ever believed possible. One woman in Kansas rushed up to me weeping and said that I had saved her life and it was the first time I had met her. Such was the response to my writing when I helped people to face their deep feelings openly and honestly. I could not write my biography without exploring that aspect of my life and experience.

My religious background was determined to take every experience in life and try to use it for a worthy purpose. It was a difficult thing to do with the most painful experiences of life, but I found that as I tried I was able to tolerate my own feelings more effectively. As I tried to help others I was not only able to help myself but I was better able to understand why that was. I was always interested in understanding the whys and wherefores of what happened to me and around me. So I made of the tragic experiences of life an active laboratory for the study of emotions and their impact on life.

It was about this time I was working as a chaplain in Memorial Hospital and got well acquainted with two researchers who were interested in cancer and its origins. One was Dr. Jerome Fredericks and the other was Dr. Lawrence LeShan. Both were deeply interested in cause-effect relationships as they were manifest in the etiology of neoplastic tissue. I had the chance to introduce these men to the pioneering work of Flanders Dunbar. Both became interested in seeing how cancer, which was considered to be the disease with no connections with an emotional etiology, was actually the best evidence for the involvement of the emotions in the origin of the disease. Dr. Fredericks was in the audience at one of my lectures on the long-term effects of emotions as a starting point for cancer. He questioned me at length on my sources and promised to keep me informed of his research. We have had a close working relationship for about thirty years. He sends me his professional papers and I often hear his lectures. As a biochemist he documents the processes at work in the body to create the precancerous tissue changes in their development. I pointed out that in working with cancer patients at Memorial Hospital I developed the practice of asking patients about the emotional crises in their lives during the period from six months to two years before the time of their diagnoses of cancer. I found that there was significant correlation though often the patients saw no connection between the incidents. Dr. Fredericks saw the chemical process that was taking place as the result of the chemical interaction and interpreted the process of tissue change. As we compared notes we were sure that we had found the missing link between the emotional cause and chemical reaction.

Dr. Fredericks tried to understand the chain of events that showed the connections between the emotions and the bodily behavior. He agreed that usually cancers started in the glands and the glands were the body system that most immediately responded to the emotions. For instance the skin with its thousands of glands is often the point of cancerous tissue developments. Fortunately it is easily observed and most accessible of the body areas and so is able to be treated successfully. Other parts of the body may be slower to reveal the neoplastic tissue developments and so may not be treated as successfully. Dr. Fredericks was able to discern the chemical changes that occurred well before they showed themselves in any major tissue changes. Because he was president of the New York Academy of Science he was in a good position to make his discoveries known.

Dr. Lawrence LeShan was a clinical and research psychologist who had been working at the Institute of Applied Biology at Trafalgar hospital. He approached the problem of cancer from a dual perspective. He was interested in the treatment and observation of individuals whom he treated. He also was concerned about what was happening in their bodies structurally as he was able to evaluate any modification of their emotional climate. We became so interested in the emotional impact on the treatment of cancer that we wrote a book together on Motivating the Life Force. Dr. LeShan and I thought it was a good book but we could not find a publisher who was willing to take the risk of publication. But the book had its value to us in the research and writing and if the world makes progress the book may eventually see the light.

Dr. LeShan worked with many cancer patients through the process of dying so that he was particularly interested in their mental processes during the final segment of life and the way their thinking contributed to their dying. Here again it was a matter of the body chemistry as it was stimulated by the thought content. Patients were able to keep up their life processes as long as they could marshal their beliefs as adequate motivation but when they lost confidence they experienced a rapid deterioration and soon were dead. It was possible to trace the loss of courage that was involved. It was possible to identify the life experience that marked the loss of faith in life and the compromise with failure and death.

My particular interest was a concern for what happened to people as a result of their experience of death, their own and those of the people who were emotionally tied to them. As a parish pastor I was in a strategic position to follow people through the process of the total encounter with the life threatening experience of their encounter with death. A person would have had to be insensitive or blind not to have seen the effect upon life. I saw several instances where a spouse died in rapid succession to the death of a husband or wife. I had the type of mind that was interested in figuring out relationships. I was interested in figuring out what made the person in acute grief vulnerable. I set up a series of evaluations of the intensity of effects and also a series of variations that could be observed. I saw the effects of acute grief with people whose lives were intimately bound together. Husbands and wives, parents and children, siblings and especially twins seemed to react most strongly. Because I was able to be with such people and talk with them quite freely I was able to put some things together in cause-effect relationships I could identify some general reactions. I saw that the amount of grief seemed to depend upon the intensity of the relationship. But there were also variables even there, for not all husband and wives, or parents and children reacted the same. What were the variables and how did they manifest themselves?

The variables were many, for no two people are alike. However, there were clearly discerned differences that could be observed. Where people poured out their feelings in an emotional overflow the acute phase of feeling seemed to be quickly managed. Where people held themselves tightly in rein and refused or were unable to express their feelings, they continued to have delayed reactions for a much longer period of time. The type of activity that they engaged in at the time of death seemed to have some bearing upon the accessibility of their feelings for active support in expressing their feelings seemed to be helpful in creating the climate for dealing with their real feelings. Any creating of an artificial climate for expressing feelings seemed to put off the expression of legitimate feeling until a less appropriate time when the stress of the emotional climate must be faced alone. It seemed to be that the more the feelings were poured out at the time of acute grief the more readily were people returned to what we may call normal. The more ceremony that channeled the feelings the more therapeutic it appeared to be.

So much has happened so quickly in the study of grief and similar emotions that it is difficult to recall the emotional climate that existed in the 1950s when I started writing on the subject. Most of the articles I wrote then have been lost with time and moving about. I never realized at the time that they would be looked back on as pioneering ventures on that subject. After writing articles mainly for church journals for several years, I tried writing a book called Understanding Grief with a subtitle, Its Roots, Dynamics and Treatment. There was no other book of its type extant so it was made up of my own original thinking and the ideas I could glean from professional journals and these were limited to say the least.

I sought out persons whom I thought had been thinking on related subjects. I was the head of a state licensed psychiatric clinic for children and their parents at the time, and we had a staff of twenty professionals. I spent quite a bit of time quizzing them about their thinking and their observations from clinical experience. I was able to talk with various members of the staff of professionals about their experiences with acute grief with children and their parents. Dr. Goodwin Watson of Columbia University was a most helpful member of the staff and I was very thankful for his wisdom and insight. Gradually from a great mass of observation and clinical experience I began to put together a philosophy of grief. In time I wrote a book dealing with different aspects of the subject. I had not planned to specialize in that material but in responding to a variety of requests my work was cut out for me. Many of these people were suffering acutely from their grief and I could not seem to refuse their anguished requests for help.

I developed the theory that acute grief was similar in its emotional impact to amputation except that one was physical and the other was emotional. Starting from there it was possible to trace the parallels as they were experienced in life. The work of Marianne Simmel of Brandeis University was most stimulating. She explored a number of variables of the experience of amputees and I compared them to the variables I observed among the grieving. We found that there are differing degrees of grief depending on the degree of emotional involvement. While there

are variations of temperament the degrees of loss depends on the emotional involvement, which is usually greatest between husband and wife,
parents and children, siblings and other relationships that are unusually
close. We also found that where there was emotional deprivation, as
among sociopaths, there was inability to feel grief in the normal sense.

About this time I began reading and talking with Dr. Erich Lindemann
who was at that time professor of Psychiatry at Harvard Medical School.
He had done important clinical and theoretical work on the subject of
grief management. I urged him to expand his articles into book length
and he responded that it was the task for younger persons to put together
what had been learned about the management of acute grief. On the
basis of his words of encouragement I began in 1955 to bring together
my thinking as it had been supplemented by a number of professionals
in the field. They are listed in the preface of the book. The book has had
an interesting history.

In 1955 I took the finished manuscript in to the office of Abingdon
Press in New York. I had not made a previous appointment. I was ushered into the regional editor who was all smiles for they had just had
agreeable acceptance of my last book on preaching. I handed him my
book on grief and without opening the book he slid it back toward me
saying that if there had been need for such a book it would have been
written long ago. I was taken back by such an absolute rejection. After
I came to myself I stammered that another publisher had asked for the
book but that I was under contract to him but if he did not want it I was
sure of another publisher. He reached across the desk for the manuscript
where he had shoved it unopened and drew it toward him with the simple
statement "I'll take it". And so he did and it went through ten printings
in 25 years and was reprinted abroad.

A number of other books by other writers and publishers followed
along in subsequent years. I was asked to write other books dealing with
other aspects of the subject. I never expected to write more than the one

book on the subject of grief and death but in time I wrote ten books that were requested. Others were asked for on children and death and one was sought on preparation for death, which became the training manual for Hospice, Inc. Probably the best known of the works was a little book that was given out by ministers and funeral directors and has been instrumental in helping many persons to accept their grief and manage it more skillfully. Similarly Fortress Press published a little book "When Someone Dies" and it has been popular with nurses who have given it to the relatives of dying patients. The popularity of the books and a newly awakened interest in the subject matter led me to make a career choice I would have been hesitant to make had my life been unstressful at the time but it seemed a good time to leave the regular parish ministry in order to fulfill the heavy demands for speaking and writing that developed with the writing of many books. So after thirty-one years in the parish I left the regular ministry to become an itinerant. Yet I served fifteen interim parishes in the next twenty years and the week before my stroke spoke six times in churches. My interest in providing a ministry to those in acute grief was not a matter of choice but I was forced into it by circumstances I could not easily control. Looking back on it now I would not have had it otherwise.

Shortly after the book Understanding Grief was published, in 1957 I went to England seeking more information about the work of that remarkable woman Cecily Saunders, M. D. She was credited as the founder and moving spirit of Hospice, Inc. Starting as a nurse she went on to get degrees in medicine and social work. In her office I was pleased to see a copy of my grief book and she seemed well acquainted with it. She was gracious and shared her work with me. We did the rounds together and talked freely of her idea of treatment. She not only sought to provide a good death but also tried to restore a good life. She admitted that not enough persons were fully restored to health but they always had that as a goal. When she spoke of restoration I was intrigued and asked if I could meet a patient who was restored to full health. She responded that

I had just been talking to such a person who went home cured and then missed the place so much that he came back to work as an orderly. I was on the organizing committee of Hospice in this country but was never able to get her broader view of treatment accepted here.

I worked for years to help get Hospice, Inc., going in this country and have had the satisfaction of seeing it become a robust institution although it is more concerned with care for the critically ill than for therapy of those whose illness is acute. For years I traveled the country and the world trying to give the message of daring care for the critically ill with the emphasis on therapy of mind and spirit for that seemed most in line with a pastor's interest. The message was like the story of the sower in the Bible for some fell on rocky soil, some among weeds, but fortunately some fell on good soil.

From what I had learned about illness, and especially cancer, it was well inside the province of pastoral care. I encouraged the use of Cecily Saunders' approach for the treatment of those afflicted. My experience was mixed. Many responded and lived on for many years and I still hear from them a couple of decades after their restoration to health. This includes some Doctors of Medicine who became interested in my emphasis. Many others failed to invest the faith and effort required, which was a dedication of life and a persistence that they were not prepared to make. But I kept at the task and finally built quite some substantial evidence of the efficacy of the method of inner discipline and serious meditation. Then I had a chance to work with myself as a test case. I had a fall with some painful results and was put through a battery of tests at the Dartmouth Medical Center. There was no permanent damage done by the fall but they found some suspicious proteins in my blood and said that it could be cancerous and would have to be carefully watched. So I took the opportunity to use myself as a guinea pig. I have practiced my type of treatment for a year and a half and have watched the suspicious protein in my blood retreat until it is no longer a threat. Fortunately I have had many years of spiritual discipline to fall back on but it has been proof that the disciplined mind and spirit can have an effect on the biological entity. Not only can the focused emotions have an effect in producing the neoplastic cells with their threat to life but they also can provide the relief in the developing cycle of controlling the developing proteins. This may be the reason why autopsies often show cancers that started and then were nipped in the bud before anyone discovered their presence. A physician who worked with cancer all his life may have been right when he said that God might be the final answer to malignancy.

For one who has directed his thought for many years toward the meaning and understanding of the impact of death upon life there are some things that have become clear with time. The unwise management of death and the attendant grief has been the cause of much human suffering. The efforts to run away from death and grief never work for one does not run away from the ultimate facts of life. The wise and open confrontation of death and grief works to take much of the fear from the subject. The mystic's effort to confront any reality brings one to place the incidents of life into the structure that looks at the experience in the larger spiritual context. People often say that the constant preoccupation with death, such as I have had for most of my life, must create a gruesome atmosphere for life. Quite the opposite seems to have been true with my life. Confrontation has taken most of the fear from the subject. Rather it is the effort to constantly look the other way that makes that other way the constant unconscious preoccupation. With Thoreau who was asked on his deathbed if he was afraid to die merely responded as he smiled to greet another friend. One of the hazards of modern life is that we hold elemental things at a distance and in the very doing of that make them more hazardous.

The wonder of creation and the place of death in the wise economy of that creation make the prospect not fearful but quite the opposite. Those who fear death tend to fear life also and move into it with apprehension. A wise appreciation of life protects it and uses its treasures wisely. When life comes to an end the mood should be less of turmoil at the inevitable than an appreciation of the wonders of life and the appreciation of its privileges. One who learns to see life and see it whole learns not so much to fear death as to look at life as a treasure to be held dear and invested with wisdom.

The mystic sees life in all its richness and wonder and uses it to make the experience of living and dying part of the same response to the God-given splendor of creation.

Chapter 19

ON BEING SPIRITUALLY CREATIVE

During the twenty years that I have been functioning as a spiritual guide primarily I have repeatedly been asked the question "How can one be creative in spiritual living?" I have avoided giving an answer because the processes involved in spiritual guidance are dialogic. But I have had a growing feeling that I should address the question knowing that any answer I would give would be partial and incomplete. Also I am well aware of the fact that we are talking about a journey and any answer would be dependent upon where we were in the venture.

I am well past my seventy-fifth milestone and that will have an effect on my answer. I have thought rather intensively about these matters for more than three score years. During much of my life I have struggled to see clearly what is involved in establishing the spiritual dimensions of life. In my writing and speaking I have hesitated to be dogmatic about my personal opinions. I have always had the opinion that spiritual con-

201

cepts were arrived at personally and shared the nature of one's own discovery so were not subject to general authority but rather were the kind of individual achievement that needed no authority but its own.

My exploration of these spiritual matters was most often shared exploration, where I was a partner in growth and birth of ideas more important to other people than to myself. That is probably the way of the spiritual guide and that is the way it should be. It is not that the ideas were unimportant, but that they were more important to the one giving birth to them than they were to the intellectual midwife. That is as it should be for there is a need to keep roles clear. So the important quest at the beginning is to discover where one is in the journey and be willing to think the thoughts and feel the feelings appropriate for the stage of the journey.

At my stage in the journey it is possible to look back with interest and appreciation at some of the milestones that seemed important at the time but have taken a secondary meaning with the passing of time and life. I can recall the times when I struggled with myself to achieve an inner discipline concerning the need to hold an idea in focus in the center of my consciousness. I know that at that state in my development it was important but now I seem to have achieved freedom from a concern about the details of discipline and have found myself at ease with the larger process within which I have become at home.

I have gone through many types of preparation for prayer. Some were primarily physical. I was concerned about getting my body into the right attitude for contemplation. I took time for preparation assuming that the time was well spent. I have worked through that phase of experience for though it may have been important at the time it no longer serves a purpose. As time went on I was aware of the fact that I was usually quite well prepared all of the time and could get about the important tasks without delay.

I have tried working with a prayer partner. Usually in college this was a short-term relationship for circumstances were constantly changing. I usually found that the process of adjustment to another was time consuming and diverting. The value was that new ideas were constantly developing and kept revealing other perspectives of prayer that were not a part of my own experience. Two novices could profitably share where they were and how they felt but this type of sharing was not as important with two disciplined practitioners.

For a variety of reasons I found that working alone was most congenial for me. This was because I developed the habit of making meditation and prayer a constant process with the shifting of prayer moods to meet the circumstances of life. I could shift from active prayer to its passive mood without making any great changes physically or mentally. I had developed the use of nonverbal forms of prayer and this facilitated the change from active to passive forms. Over the years I found that the process was little disrupted by shifting from active to passive. In fact the whole day was never far from the focus of the prayerful though its activity might be quite varied. From early morning to late at night the basic focus remained much the same and the prayerful attitude remained much the same though the active element of life varied. This kind of focus on prayer was one that could not be shared easily for the activity had to be controlled by carefully learned inner disciplines.

The active phase of prayer called for a constant effort at centering. Early in the learning process I made a vigorous discipline of consciously seeking to hold one thought in the center of my awareness. This practice of centering is not designed to banish from your mental activity all thoughts that are inimical to prayerful activity but rather to protect the central purpose of prayer. Prayer is a singular activity freeing the spirit to soar to heights of mystical perception. It does not deny the intellect but it is more than an activity of the mind. It moves into overdrive the processes of mind, for it adds another dimension to the usual thought processes. It establishes active partnership with the spiritual beings past

203

and present that examine the depths and heights of the explorations of the human boundaries of consciousness.

Centering involves concentration as a first step. I well remember some of the methods I used at the beginning to gain some facility with the discipline of the mind. I went to college in that part of the country where basketball is king. I would go to the basketball game and use the game and the surrounding frenzy as part of my discipline. I made a pact with myself to focus my mind in undiverted attention of my studies for the first half of the game. If I was successful in my self-discipline for that part then I was free to enjoy the game with its excitement the second half. It was a difficult task to hold my mind to its task even though the crowd was cheering and the atmosphere was charged with emotion. However, It was a useful device for I learned to concentrate so completely that nothing that was going on around me was able to penetrate my centering until I gave it permission to do so. Once I learned the discipline it served me in good stead for the rest of my life. The next stage was to use the centering for worthy purpose.

It was at that time we studied in philosophy the meaning of transcendence. I put the idea of transcendence to work in my thinking of God. Prayer was a relationship with God so it had to be a process of mind and spirit that could be employed much the same as centering. Of course its purpose was different but its use of mental techniques was comparable. Knowledge was an important part of transcendence. That was the intellectual part of the relationship and it used all of the attributes of mind to further the perception of the nature of God. The more you know and the more you seek to know the more your knowledge of God grows. The counterpart is your feeling for God, which comes from the cultivation of the sense of awe and wonder that is enhanced by the feeling relationship with God. Both the growth of the mind and spirit can be cultivated with all of the capacity of mind and emotion of which the person is capable. The wise balance of mind and emotion is essential to the healthy growth of the transcendent capacity.

The process by which mind and emotion are cultivated is familiar to the philosophical growth of spiritual awareness. As knowledge and cultivated feeling grows so does the perception of the nature and perception of God become more compelling. To use an illustration of the process, a child is taught that God is an all-pervading reality. This is both reassuring and a cause of fright. It is a concept incorporated at the level of the child's experience. Unless the child's idea grows it may be made a part of life in an inappropriate way. The fear may grow and the assurance may be overwhelmed. Then the religion of the child may be seriously warped and a small idea of God may stand in the way of achieving the benefits of real transcendence.

However, the growing consciousness may develop to another level of perception. As an adolescent the child may have a growing awareness of a cosmic force that is both rational and benevolent in its use of power. It may be quite satisfied with that idea of God and may go through the years content with the idea that seemed to satisfy both the intellectual and emotional needs, until a crisis develops which places an excessive strain upon life. In the crisis the inclination is either to grow rapidly to new and more mature concepts or reject the whole idea as unworthy of the mature thinking the crisis demands. Often the middle life crisis involves the need to grow a more adequate perception of God or suffer the consequences. There may follow a time of rapid growth and fulfillment or the movement into a state of mind and emotion that may plague the rest of life with depression and dark thoughts and unfulfilled feelings.

Often this is the time of life where the growth of mind and spirit comes to fulfillment and a transcendent way of looking at life may be achieved. Often this is the experience of those who are called saints who go into a period of spiritual overdrive where they seem to achieve a special relationship with God that is personally fulfilling. This is where the mind and emotion of the person finds a relationship with the mind and spirit of Cosmic Person that bridges the gap of creation and makes it possible for creature and creator to move beyond the limits that are posed by creatureliness to find that unity in spirit for which the earth-bound yearn.

How then may the human find that spiritually creative dimension of being that St. Augustine sought and for which so many yearn? It may be the object of seeking and yet it does not come by seeking alone. Some have sought it endlessly to no avail. Others find it seemingly without seeking. We are dealing here with an element of uncertainty. There seems to be a necessity in these things for a calm openness for the spiritual life is not forced or compelled. It is necessary to believe it can happen. There is an availability that may possess life and a constant seeking that is an invitation. The mystic lives with the awareness of the various stages that lead to a warming of the spirit. The process of prayer is an opening of self that in a sense always has the welcome mat out. We are not always fully aware of the movement of the inner being. It is aware of its own need and the process of its seeking but it is not sure of how it may share in the fulfilling of the moments of opportunity.

There are moments when the seeking takes on the mood of desperation and then not much is accomplished. The creativity comes through times when the inner being is able to be both relaxed and expectant at the same time. In music the violinist is in mastery of his instrument and sure of his interpretation when something happens and the artist and the instrument come together in a mystical unity which completes them both. This is the fulfilling of much practice and discipline. Nothing is added that did not seem to be there before and yet it is obvious that something new is there. A mystical achievement has been added. An artist before a canvas ignites a perception and it in a moment becomes something new. So the person in prayer is aware of something new that touches life with creativity. In responding to it a new mastery of life is experienced. He hasn't compelled anything but he has been compelled by it. He has been responsive to something beyond mere circumstance. He has allowed the power of God to show itself through his praying self.

At the moment of mystical unity he knows that he is more than he was but he cannot describe it. It may change his life so completely that everything before this moment fades into insignificance and everything that happens from then on is different because this moment of illumination has occurred. He has been centered and he has been involved in transcendence. But this stretched his capacity to comprehend and explain. He lets it go as one of those things that surpass time and understanding. He can testify but he cannot explain for what has happened with him is more than he can comprehend.

Sometimes the best evidence of the significance of the change wrought by the spiritual view within is shown by the way the person responds to the circumstances of life. This is sometimes shown by the person's response to physical crises. As a byproduct of the spiritual change there may be a significant modification in the quality of life. At times this manifests itself in physical changes either in the capacity to endure or in the apparent altering of the physical circumstances of life. Other evidences of important changes within the person may be shown in major modifications in the personality. The person who was quick to complain and intolerant of others may become able to endure hardship without complaint. The physical condition may remain unchanged as far as any observation is concerned but the internal climate is vastly different.

Sometimes the evidence of spiritual changes takes place without any visible show. The person who has had an illumination does not want acclaim or approval but quietly gives an indication that things within are different and much better. This type of person shows the effects of spiritual change in different ways. The creativity within the spiritual life is in keeping with the major traits of the person. Demonstrative people will be showing their feelings while withdrawn persons will continue to be more secretive. But the changes will be real and observable.

In the quiet moments of prayer important things may happen, so the mood of expectancy is always appropriate. The deliberate effort to set mind and spirit free of the turmoil of life is made with purpose. The effort to seek an important center for being is compatible with an ease of the inner climate that is conducive to transcendence. The person in prayer is giving an invitation to a cosmic counterpart to enter into a relationship that may bear fruit in new and surpassing awareness. It is important that this awareness be the product of a mind and spirit that is expectant. In the quiet depths of being, the seeker in prayer dares to challenge the limits of humanity by an approach to divinity. Accepting the daring idea of being made in the divine image and acting upon that audacious attempt to prove the validity of that assumption is basic to our concept of our divine relationship.

We are not naive. We know that our earth has four billion souls seeking meaning for life. We know that our universe is but one of billions that share the life of this wonderful creation. If we seek a special relationship with a cosmic entity that will give us special privilege we are bound to be disappointed. But there are four billion people on this earth each one breathing a share of its oxygen and thus sustaining life. It is personalized as it is used. So in claiming a share of God it is personalized and given a new meaning for life. As we enter into prayer we work with our own share of infinity. As our lungs share the oxygen of the atmosphere, so life sustaining for us, so our spiritual achievement is making our share of God viable to the centering and transcendence we would experience.

It is interesting that science is coming to some of the same conclusions. I have been working in recent years with Henry Margenau, Sterling professor of Physics at Yale. He is thought by many to be the outstanding philosopher of science in our day. He points out that the explorations of science are for all practical purposes blocked by the boundaries that science encounters as it pursues its explorations further and further in the direction of the infinitely large and the infinitesimally small. Boundaries become confounding for they point out the limits of our methods of inquiry but also our limited equipment for understanding. We run out of areas of certainty and must settle for probability that may vary while we are exploring. During a carefully monitored experiment we traveled to the boundaries of usually accepted scientific judgments and then moved out into the realm of the uncertain and the experimental. Here he admitted that the modes of judgment had to be less scientific and more a product of spiritual hunches. And what is more he was willing to put it in writing.

It becomes more reasonable all the time to look inward for the realities of life. It is reasonable for us to look for the certainties of life at the point where science and philosophy meet. This does not mean a capitulation to those so-called fundamentalists who sell their brain short by a quick agreement with the Bible. Rather it means using the best insight of research and science to arrive at an understanding of how wise religion and wise science can come to an understanding of man and nature as elements of a creative concept of purpose.

The disciplined consciousness will undoubtedly play an important part in this quest. There is no more creative use of the spiritual potential of human being and the power found there than accepting the guidance of that power during these trying days.

Chapter 20

To Be Continued

As I contemplated this last chapter of my personal opus I had thought of calling it "and in summary", or "and in conclusion". I mentioned it to my friend Pen Dimock. She took exception to that title and said "I can't really imagine you at the conclusion of anything. You would always find another dimension to explore". I had to admit that at that point she knew me better than I knew myself.

There is a sense in which a mystic never admits that anything is marked by definite boundaries. Everything has more to it than is first seen. The mystic is characterized by a never-ending belief or imagination that refuses to set the limits of life or experience because there is always more to the experience than can be defined or explained. What seems to be the end may in truth be but another beginning. I have had that experience often in life. When I had thought I had worked out a vein of experience and was ready to turn elsewhere I found that it was really at a new beginning. The discovery of the yet to be known was a challenging new part of life.

I was recently going over a student's effort to write out her philosophy of life. It was carefully thought out and I found myself in agreement with nearly everything. But she said, "When this life is over that's it. There isn't anything else". I questioned her about this conclusion and she responded with the usual string of negations. There was no room in her thinking for any really adventurous ideas. She had pulled the curtain of disbelief down tight around herself and there was no room left for the great possibilities in her unexplored territory of mind or soul. She didn't want to contemplate such things for she had already given the negative answer and there was no room for exploratory thinking.

I remembered some of the experiences I had had when I was working with Eileen Garrett as a part time consultant. My friend Larry LeShan had talked to her about me and my way of thinking and she thought I would be a good person to invite into the Parapsychology Foundation. So it was that I was welcomed aboard and I found one of the most interesting groups of people I had ever had anything to do with. Most of them were scientists of the physical or personality type. Their approach was open and honest. They shared the basic and unfettered viewpoint of the traditional mystic and I soon felt quite at home among them.

One day I went into Dr. LeShan's office and he said "Did you notice those two women in the office with Mrs. Garrett?" I said I had. One was middle aged and the other one was younger. Dr. LeShan explained that one was the wife and the other the daughter of a prominent physician who had been elected mayor of a large western city. Then he explained that they were there on a strange mission. They wanted information about their husband and father and they were seeking it through Mrs. Garrett who was a well-known psychic sensitive.

Then he related the following sequence of events. Some time before they had been in for a session in which he, Dr. LeShan, was involved as the recorder of what happened. He acted as the master of ceremonies, so to speak, and ran the tape recorder. Mrs. Garrett went into a deeply altered state of consciousness. Soon thereafter she began to speak in a markedly altered manner. The women quickly recognized it as their husband and father who had died several years before. In their devoted effort to write his biography they were confounded by several years of missing data. It was recommended that they seek the help of Mrs. Garrett.

Little did they expect such a sharp rebuke. He berated them for their ineptness. He said if they knew him at all they would have known what he thought. He told them that the documents and scholarly papers they wanted were all in boxes stored in the room over the garage. He went on for a considerable time and it was getting near the end of the tape. Dr. LeShan warned him that it was near the end of the interview but he argued that he had wanted to get to these women for a long time and he was not about to cut off his comments. He was told it was not good for Mrs. Garrett to be in the altered state of consciousness too long. He argued that as a physician he knew what was good for her. He was finally told that when the tape ended so did the interview. The tape began to flap and Mrs. Garrett returned to waking consciousness.

Dr. LeShan told me that he was pretty well shaken up by the encounter. He said he went down to the bar on the first floor of the building on 57th street. He said it is quite a strain to carry on an argument with somebody who has been dead a few years.

One cannot easily practice denial on some human experiences. The fact that they are surrounded by safeguards of a scientific nature makes them even less accessible to easy methods of getting around them. If you should want to explore things of this type in a serious and scholarly form you might read The Medium, The Mystic And The Physicist by Dr. Lawrence LeShan, which has more about Mrs. Garrett and is dedicated to me.

212

Incidentally when they searched for the lost documents they were all where he told them they would be. This day they were back for another session seeking information for the husband and physician's biography or autobiography, as you may want to call it. Dr. LeShan was wondering what would be his experience presiding at the tape recorder.

It is usually assumed that scientists and scientifically trained persons such as physicians are trustworthy witnesses to the phenomena that speak of another dimension of human experience. My daughter knowing of my interest in such things brought me a book recently by a Swedish psychiatrist named Nils O. Jacobson called <u>Life Without Death</u>.

Dr. Jacobson had made a careful study of the things that are usually carefully ignored by people in their ordinary, every day lives. He approached them skeptically but had to admit that even from the purely scientific viewpoint there was much that could not be reasonably ignored. The mystical view of life gave experience and information not easily found in the casual daily life of most humans. He pursued these experiences and information and believed that he discovered a dimension of life that was beyond the common boundaries usually attributed to life. In fact he believed that a person could learn how to live beyond the experience of death as commonly encountered by finding the method of keeping consciousness alive after the physical brain has disintegrated in physical death. His book outlines the way he approaches this discovery and explains the title of his book.

Dr. Robert Laidlaw carried the search a step farther for he actually carried out a psychiatric intervention on a man who supposedly died during the American Revolution. The process involved was documented with tape recordings in a book called <u>Beyond The Five Senses</u> by Eileen Garrett and published by Helix Press. Robert Laidlaw was chief of psychiatry at Roosevelt Hospital in New York. I knew him well because we had served together on National committees, the National Council of Churches Committee on Religion and Medicine and the Planned

Parenthood Committee on Education for Marriage. I had watched him at work in these committees and trusted the way his mind worked. He was professionally involved in an unusual case that I will describe:

The editor of the Daily News, the largest selling paper in New York, had bought a lovely estate up the Hudson about half way to Albany. He and his family had moved in, but that was the beginning of the trouble. Every night about midnight there were noises so distressing that they ended sleep and soon the family abandoned the main house and moved into the gate house pending the resolution of the noise problem. Carpenters and plumbers searched in vain for an explanation of the trouble. Electricians did the same.

Finally in desperation the editor consulted Dr. Laidlaw to see if he could throw light on the matter. After considering the matter and getting all the information possible the Doctor decided that it called for personal investigation. So they made an appointment to drive up to the estate some evening after work and personally scout out the place and its noises.

On the appointed evening the editor and his chauffeur, a reporter who was an expert in tape recorders, Mrs. Garrett and Dr. Laidlaw set out for the pleasant drive up the Hudson to the estate in question. When they arrived at the abandoned house they set up the tape recorder and made themselves at home and comfortable. They explored the premises and then seated themselves in a living room to await developments. At about midnight they began to hear noises of digging and moving of heavy objects.

Dr. Laidlaw who had worked with Mrs. Garrett many times before said that it was time for her to go into her altered state of consciousness, which she did. After she seemed to be in a deep state Dr. Laidlaw addressed the source of the noise and after awhile got a response in an archaic dialect of German. Dr. Laidlaw had been partially educated in Germany so that he was able to carry on a conversation with the entity.

It appeared that the disembodied entity was a Hessian soldier who had been executed by the British during the Revolution for being a traitor. Dr. Laidlaw and the Hessian soldier carried on quite a conversation. The soldier appeared to have no knowledge of the passing of time and was trying to find some papers hidden under the porch. The porch had been altered many times in the two hundred or so years that had intervened. The papers could not be found and so the soldier's frustration lasted on and on.

Then it was that Dr. Laidlaw tried to explain to the soldier what had happened. He led him to see that those who accused him were long gone and that there was no one left to accuse him. The Hessian soldier was told that he could go on about whatever cosmic journey pleased him but he needed to continue his earthly search no longer.

The account in the book referred to was much longer than our account and you are referred to it for details. The substance of the account is that there was no more disturbance in the house and the family moved back into its spacious quarters to enjoy the undisturbed peacefulness.

The important thing from our perspective is that the life of the consciousness seems to have no sense of time and what has happened two hundred years ago is very much alive in an injured consciousness or whatever portion of it still is functioning. Also there is evidence that the sensitivity of the psyche can affect the remnant of the person for untold time. Much of the experience may show up in two largely incompatible dimensions.

I have read largely in the literature of the Society of Psychical Research and have been influenced by the vast quantity of research that seems to be sound and valid. I do not think it can be ignored. Anyone who wants to be responsive to the total phenomena that have to do with the human spirit cannot act as if this body of knowledge did not exist. Some of the things that have happened to me are in that category of the difficult to explain.

My wife and I decided to take a conducted tour by bus through Arizona. The tour director had a session with all the members of the trip describing the rules and regulations. He explained that there would be a valuable prize offered to the one who guessed the total mileage of the trip when concluded. A number immediately jumped into my mind. I told it to my wife and she made a note of it. I gave it no more thought and did not try to calculate anything. At the end we turned in our numbers. Mine was right on the nose and my wife was second prize. I was embarrassed and tried to reject the prize because I had had cosmic help and the director said, "Don't be crazy". That is how my efforts to recognize another dimension in my mental life have been greeted so that I have usually found that it is better to keep such things to myself.

But in this effort to look at my life from a total perspective I want to recognize this something else. Dr. LeShan told me that I was the only person he knew who lives completely in the two realities, the material and the extrasensory. I have my doubts about that but I am quite sure that sixty five years given to extensive meditation have made it possible for me to develop an ability to shift from one level of consciousness to another with alacrity. I know that in altering my state of consciousness, as I do in healing intervention, I move from ordinary consciousness into what I call the special state almost instantly. There was a time when it took a lot more time and effort. Yet it never seems to put me in any jeopardy for I can also return to ordinary awareness just as readily. Maybe the borderline has been worn down with extensive use and is not so formidable with mine as with some people.

I do think that attitude is crucial. If a person wants to develop a quality of mind, willing can have an important part in achieving it. I remember reading a book by Gertrude Shmeidler and R. A. McConnell called Extrasensory Perception And Personality Patterns, Yale University Press. It made quite an impression on me because it started out as their effort to disprove the phenomena of another reality. Shmeidler was a psychologist and McConnell was a mathematician-physicist. They found what they read about psychic phenomena and extrasensory perception disturbed them and their worldview rather badly so they united their efforts to obliterate once and for all that kind of thinking. They devised extensive experiments that would fulfill their purpose. They set to work at their project. The only thing was that the more they experimented the more they seemed to prove the opposite of what they sought. So they had to stop and reevaluate their findings. Their book was eventually published to support the exact opposite thesis, that there was another dimension that they had to explore.

One of these theses was that attitude determines outcome in parapsychological experiments. For instance when they tried research with people that believed in extrasensory perception they found that they were positive in both their belief and their research findings. Also they found that when they did experiments with people who did not believe in the paranormal or extrasensory perception they did not find any belief but instead they found a negative response. And what was also true and quite significant was that the amount of the negative and positive responses were almost identical, the same amount above and below chance. This was the first time that they had gotten proof in the laboratory that both faith and doubt were measurable. There had been many instances where it had been a reasonable assumption that attitudes were measurable but here was the laboratory measurement.

Dr. R. W. Bucke, a Canadian psychiatrist, had a mystical experience quite unexpectedly one evening that produced major changes in his life. He saw all at once the meaning of life and all the puzzling aspects of his experience were suddenly made clear. He spent the rest of his life in the glow of these few moments trying to interpret for others the nature and meaning of the mystical experience. The book he wrote, Cosmic Consciousness, has become a classic.

Even more startling discoveries are reported in France and reprinted in the journal Nature. It seems that the electrical signature can remain after the substance has been reduced as much as one hundred and twenty times. It has been assumed in previous scientific study that it is essential for molecules to be present to make it possible, for instance, for a serum to have effectiveness. But now it seems that the serum can be reproduced from the moleculeless electrical signature. They open new doors in medical research for, in AIDS for instance, it was impossible to make a vaccine that did not carry the disease in a person with a destroyed resistance. Already there have been experiments with new vaccines that are made using only the electrical signature. These appear to be effective.

These new insights about electrical signatures without molecules not only have interesting possibilities about medical problems. They also open up new possibilities about the nature of human beings. It makes possible new conditions for the traits of humans who have been puzzled by the nature of consciousness. We have long been troubled by the relationship of consciousness and brain function. Now it seems as if the products of mental life can be seen as a possibility without a molecular base. This gives a reality to nonmaterial dimensions that was not known before. Not only does this discovery give new possibilities to scientific exploration, but it also makes the actions of consciousness and religious discovery a new validity. The reason scientists are so concerned about such new factors to be considered is that they may make insecure the basis of materialism and much of the assumed nature of science. There is no end of the effect of these considerations for our long accepted worldview.

As I approach the beginning of my ninth decade, many of the thoughts that have intrigued me for most of my life are gaining new relevance. It is no longer necessary for us to think of the mystical awareness and cosmic consciousness as the territory for way out thinkers. They are becoming the place where science is struggling with frontier thoughts and related explorations. With new relevance advanced thinkers have to consider possibilities that were not thought of as the province of understanding explorers. As the mystics look at the world that is being revealed it is possible to see infinite new horizons and to feel perfectly at home in the world that is emerging.

When we look back at the century that is ending we can see marvelous changes taking place. More scientific development has taken place than ever before in history. When we look forward into the next century we can but dimly glimpse what will happen. With my lifelong interest in science and mysticism I may have foreseen the amalgamation of two streams of thought that have unlimited power to shape the destiny of human kind. It will be a great future and I trust I will see or feel it from afar.

Afterword and Editor's Notes

Other than correcting a few typos I have tried to keep this work as Dad wrote it. It is not a typical autobiography. It charts a spiritual journey rather than enumerating activities and accomplishments. He wasn't one for tooting his own horn. He minimized many of his achievements and graciously allowed others to receive credit for his work. He was a 'behind the scenes' kind of person who never sought the limelight. Author Larry LeShan recounted that often a box of books would arrive at his door and he would look them over, wonder why Edgar had sent them, and shove them off in a corner. Then he would come to an impasse in research he was doing, or encounter a new situation and remember seeing something about that in one of those books. He said that Edgar was always a step ahead, even when Larry, himself, wasn't sure which direction he was headed.

I would like to thank the Revs. John Carr and C. Ray Stephens for their contributions.

John graduated from Ohio Wesleyan University in 1953 and received his Bachelor of Divinity degree from Yale Divinity School in 1957. John was ordained into the New York Annual Conference of the United Methodist Church as an elder and full member in 1957. He served as an associate pastor at Westbury, Long Island and then as pastor at Hauppauge, Long Island, 1958-63, and Faith United Methodist in North Haven, CT from 1963-66. In 1966, he began training as a hospital chaplain at Yale New Haven Hospital and became a supervisor in Clinical Pastoral Education (CPE) in 1970. During his 30 years as a CPE supervisor, while employed in the Department of Religious Ministries and Yale New Haven Hospital, John supervised students at the Connecticut Mental Health Center, Gaylord Hospital in Wallingford, Yale New Haven Hospital, and the Yale Psychiatric Hospital. During his early chaplaincy training, John received a Master of Sacred Theology from Yale Divinity School in 1967. In the early '70's he was a lecturer for a few years at the Yale Divinity School, teaching a course called personal counseling and crisis ministry.

John was assigned to the United Methodist delegation to the Council on Church Union (COCU) in the late '70's and served as co-chair on the COCU Task Force on Disabled Persons. He also served two terms as chair of the Eastern Region of the Association of Clinical Pastoral Education (ACPE) and one term on the ACPE Ethics Commission.

John was a New York Annual Conference delegate to the Northeastern Jurisdiction in 1984, 1988, and 1992 and was a member of the General Board of Higher Education and Ministry from 1988 until 1996. During these same eight years, he served on the United Methodist Endorsing Committee for those entering extension ministries.

John served for four years as chair of the Connecticut Coalition of Citizens with Disabilities, a statewide cross-disability advocacy group. He also served for several years as a Governor-appointed member of the Governor's Committee for Employment of People with Disabilities. For several years in the late '80's he served as chair of the Accessibility Committee in the New York Annual Conference of the United Methodist Church.

John retired from full-time ministry in 1997 and for the past ten years has served part-time as the executive director of a national caucus, the Association of Physically Challenged Ministers of the United Methodist Church.

John has written for several newspapers and magazines and has a chapter called "Searching for the Boundaries" in a book entitled *Coping with Crisis and Handicap*, Plenium Press, edited by Aubrey Milansky (1981).

He is married to Maggie has two children, David and Karen, and five grandchildren, Brendan, Noah, Caeli, Joshua, and Nathaniel.

Rev. Dr. C. Ray Stephens is an ordained minister of the United Methodist Church. He served United Methodist Churches until he went into the army as a chaplain in 1967. He became a CPE supervisor while in the army and has served in this capacity since 1972. In addition, he had a five year assignment as Director of holistic medicine at the Walter Reed Army Medical Center in Washington D.C.

Letter sent to friends and family on April 17, 1994

Dear Friends:

We are writing to let you know that Edgar, our beloved husband and father, died Friday April 15 at home with us in Corinth Corners. We are saddened by his passing, but we rejoice with him that he is finally free of the body which served him less and less well over the years since his stroke. In the last few months his condition deteriorated rapidly and he was confined to his bed for the last three weeks. Throughout it all he retained his sense of humor and his caring and compassion for others. He continued his active life of prayer and meditation even when communication with us became difficult. He maintained a sense of connection to so many of you that he had met through his teaching, writing and travels. He died at 6:30 a.m. and we notified only the doctor, the Funeral Director, and our Visiting Nurse. But by 8:30 a.m. the phone had begun to ring. People were calling spontaneously from all over the country; "I've been thinking about Edgar for two days", "I can't get Edgar out of my mind, tell me what's happening" and other statements of the kind. We had the sense that he took some time to bid a number of farewells. We hope that you will continue to feel that he is a part of your life, helping you through the rough spots as he often did. A Service of Remembrance will be held at 7:00 PM on Saturday, May 7th at the United Church of Chelsea, VT. In lieu of flowers, contributions can be made to the Visiting Nurse Alliance of Vermont and New Hampshire,

PO Box 157, Bradford, VT 05033; Hospice of the Upper Valley, RR4 Box 325, Lebanon, NH 03766 or to the charity of your choice.

The In Memoriam written for the New York Conference Journal

The Reverend Edgar Newman Jackson, D.D. died Friday April 15, 1994 at his home in Corinth Corners, Vermont. "Edgar was one of my models for ministry; he befriended and supported me in so many ways. I have wonderful memories of our years at Shelter Island. Through his writing and lecturing he supported and stimulated a host of people." Rev. Matthew Gates. "Certainly, Edgar was one of the great intellects and magnificent spirits of the second half of the twentieth century." Rev. Joel Warner, Pastor, Lake Ronkonkoma UMC. "I shall greatly miss Ed... he was the kind of Christian minister I had always hoped to be. In his shared insights and concerns, I came to appreciate the exceptional abilities and Christian dedication that characterized all of Ed's ministry. I thank God for his books, his service to the church and to so many needful individuals over the years. He has left both fond memories and thoughts in his many books that will long outlive him in continuing his ministry." Rev. Lester Loder, Saranac Lake, NY

Born July 8, 1910, the son of the Rev. Edgar Starkey and Abbie (Newman) Jackson in Cold Spring Harbor, New York. In 1932 he graduated from Ohio Wesleyan University where he later also received his Doctorate of Divinity. He continued his studies at Drew University, Union, the Divinity School and the William Allison White School of Psychotherapy at Yale (BD & MDiv), Columbia, the Postgraduate Center for Psychotherapy, and Oxford University. On June 12, 1934, he married Estelle Miller. They had three children, Edgar Duval Jackson (1935-1936), James Ward Jackson (1938-1972) and Lois E. Jackson of Chelsea, VT.

His Father and Grandfather were both Methodist ministers. Dr. Robert Fulton of the University of Minnesota said, "He had a family tradition of service to his faith and he brought to the study of death and grief a towering and disciplined intellect as well as a compassionate heart. His pioneering book, Understanding Grief, was a call to action that gave birth to the 'death awareness' movement in the U.S. It not only laid the groundwork for our present understanding of grief and how we might cope with it, but also brought attention to the manner in which our society denied both the prospect and the reality of death. Because Edgar lived, thousands of men and women across this country—indeed throughout the world—have found solace in their grief and renewed faith in life."

Dr. Jackson was a member of the New York East, and New York conferences of the United Methodist Church and served parishes in Centerport NY 1934-36, Thomaston, CT 1936-40, Park Church, New Haven, CT 1940-42, Winsted, CT 1942-44, Chaplain, US Army Air Corps 1944-46, Newfield Church, Bridgeport, CT 1946©51, Mamaroneck, NY 1952©63 & 1964. His years in the Mamaroneck Methodist Church were a time of tremendous growth in that parish. The church grew physically through addition of a Christian Education building and increased membership. It grew spiritually through prayer groups and healing services, which helped to redefine the boundaries of the Christian community. In 1965 he left the parish ministry and served in a supernumerary capacity and in 1969 he retired. From 1965-83 Dr. Jackson served as an interim minister in Chelsea, Bethel, Rochester, East Barnard, St. Johnsbury, Thetford, Rutland, Fairlee, & Randolph, Vermont. During this time, he was also a visiting professor at The University of Minnesota, St. John's University, The New England Institute, and served as a consultant in crisis psychology at the Walter Reed Medical School.

Nominated by members of the Dartmouth Medical School Faculty, he was chosen as an Outstanding Educator of 1972. He has lectured at colleges, universities, and medical schools, as well as professional conferences and seminars throughout the United States and abroad. He was included in "Who's Who In The East" and "Who's Who In Education". In 1979 he received the Distinguished Service Award from the New England Institute of Applied Sciences in Boston, MA.

He served as a Chaplain in the Army Air Corps in WWII, and immediately following the war served on the Secretariat of the Vatican working in the distribution of relief supplies in Italy. Since that time he has continued to serve as a Technical Advisor to the Air Force, lecturing to chaplain's groups and assisting in the development of crisis management techniques.

Dr. Jackson, who has been called "the outstanding authority of our time on crisis management", authored more than 40 books on personal and group counseling. His pioneering work, 'Understanding Grief', published in 1957 and considered a classic in its field, laid the groundwork for the current approaches to grief and grief management. In this and many of his 45 succeeding books including; "Understanding Loneliness", "Understanding Prayer", "Coping with the Crises in Your Life", "Counseling the Dying", "You & your Grief", "Your Health and You", "Though We Suffer", and "Telling A Child About Death", his basic concern was to interpret the research of the personality sciences for use by members of the care-taking professions.

He was also the author of "Green Mountain Hero", an historical novel about the early history of Vermont recently republished by New England Press.

Dr. Jackson has served as a member of several national organizations in the care-taking professions. He has been a consultant for national committees such as the National Cancer Institute, National Funeral Director's Association, National Planned Parenthood, and the National Council of Churches. His early work with Dame Cecily Saunders of Great Britain helped to establish the Hospice movement in this country.

He was a healer. Through individual and group counseling and laying on of hands, he performed healing interventions in thousands of cases throughout the world. A stroke suffered in 1983 curtailed his travel and lecture activities, but he continued to write, authoring "Understanding Health", "Conquering Disability", and this autobiography, and to host conferences in his home through 1991.

My Eulogy for Edgar

At his memorial service, I read Robert Frost's poem, "The Road Less Traveled".

My father took the road less traveled by. And it was never the easy road. He never simply accepted rules, doctrines or dogma, but always asked why. Not from plain feistiness, but from the desire to always do more than he was asked and to find a way to do it better.

He listened. He had a knack for hearing not just the words, but also the true substance behind the words so that many times he defined and met our needs before we even recognized them.

He read. He read constantly and voraciously and he remembered everything and its source and he assimilated it all into a body of knowledge that was astounding.

He wrote. He took the things he read and those that he observed and put them together in new, exciting, and challenging ways and shared them with us through more than 40 books.

He laughed. He had a ready wit and helped us find the humor in many situations. In his pain of the last few years he still laughed easily and joked with all of us to lighten our burden of caring for him.

He loved. He loved each of us unconditionally. Even when we disappointed him his love helped us find ways to be better people.

He died. And in his death he has shown us that the spirit and love live on. His spirit was too big and too vital for the frail body that could no longer contain it. He is now a part of the mind of God.

The End

Publications List – Edgar N. Jackson		
1947	This is My Faith	Board of Education, Methodist Church, Abingdon Press
1951	God Can Heal You Now	Guideposts
1954	How to Preach to People's Needs	Abingdon, Baker Book House 1970-1-2-3-4
1957	Understanding Grief	Abingdon (10 printings), SCM Press—London (paperback)
1958	Facing Ourselves	with Russell Dicks, Abingdon Press, Nashville
1958	Fronteer Teen-age Stories	Lantern Press
1959	Grief and Religion	In Meaning of Death , Herman Feifel, Ed., McGraw-Hill, NY
1961	You and Your Grief	Channel Press (25 printings), Round Table Press—Mass sales, Hawthorn Press (12 printings), E.P. Dutton, Epworth Press, London (paperback)
1961	A Psychology for Preaching	Channel Press, Hawthorn Press, Harper's Minister's Paperback Library
1961	Green Mountain Hero	Lantern Press, New England Press (paperback)
1963	For the Living	Channel Press (300,000 first run, many reprints), Des Moines

1963	The Pastor and His People	Channel Press, Hawthorne Press
1963	Understanding Prayer	W. Clement Stone, NY SCM, London 1980, World Press, Cleveland Fortress Press, Philadelphia, Harper and Row
1964	Explaining Death to Children	Beacon Press
1965	Telling a Child About Death	Channel Press, NY
1966	The Christian Funeral	Channel Press, NY
1966	The Significance of the Christian Funeral	National Funeral Directors Association
1967	Growth through Grief	Forest Hospital, Des Plains, Ill,
1968	Youth and the Funeral	Wisconsin Seminar Publication
1968	When Someone Dies	Fortress Press, Philadelphia
1969	Group Counseling	Pilgrim Press, Philadelphia
1969	Why You Should Understand Grief: A Minister's View	In But Not to Lose, Kutscher, Ed, Frederick Fell, NY
1969	Attitudes toward Death in our Culture	in Death and Bereavement, Kutscher, Ed, Charles C. Thomas, Springfield, IL
1970	Counseling the Dying	With James Knight & Lawrence LeShan, Thomas Nelson, Hawthorn, Jason Aronson, Harper and Row

1970	Though We Suffer	United Methodist Publishing House, Nashville
1971	Cuanco Alguien Muere	Buenos Aires, Argentina
1972	Body Image and Grief Response	In Religion and Bereavement, Kutscher, Ed, Health Sciences Publishing Corp., NY
1972	Helping Children Cope With Death	In Religion and Bereavement, Kutscher, Ed, Health Sciences Publishing Corp., NY
1972	The Importance of Understanding Grief	In Religion and Bereavement, Kutscher, Ed, Health Sciences Publishing Corp., NY
1972	A Pastoral Call Following Death	In Religion and Bereavement, Kutscher, Ed, Health Sciences Publishing Corp., NY
1972	Suspended Death	In Religion and Bereavement, Kutscher, Ed, Health Sciences Publishing Corp., NY
1972	Understanding the Teenagers Response to Death	In Religion and Bereavement, Kutscher, Ed, Health Sciences Publishing Corp., NY
1972	What is Happening to Feelings?	In Religion and Bereavement, Kutscher, Ed, Health Sciences Publishing Corp., NY

1973	Catastrophic Illness	Cancer Care, 25th Anniversary lecture, NY
1973	Counseling in Funeral Service	Textbook, New England Institute
1973	Coping with the Crises in Your Life	Jason Aronson, NY, Hawthorn, NY
1973	Understanding Grief	In Pastoral Care of the Dying and Bereaved: Selected Readings, Robert Reeves, ED, Health Sciences Publishing Corp
1974	Sociologia de la Muerte	Madrid
1974	The Condolence Letter	In Concerning Death, Earl Grollman, Ed, Beacon Press, Boston
1974	Grief	In Concerning Death, Earl Grollman, Ed, Beacon Press, Boston
1975	Parish Counseling	Jason Aronson, NY,
1975	Wise Management of Grief	In Grief and the Meaning of the Funeral, Otto Margolis, MSS Information Group, NY
1977	Living with Death	Christian Education Council of South Australia
1977	The Many Faces of Grief	SCM, London; Abingdon Press, Nashville;, Thomas Nelson; Harper and Row
1979	Bereavement and Grief	In Dying: Facing the Facts, Hannelore Wass, Ed., Hemisphere Publishing Co., Washington, NY,

1980	Understanding Loneliness	SCM, London, Fortress Press, Philadelphia
1980	The Shadow of Death	NFDA
1981	Living till we Die	Published proceedings and lectures,, So. Carolina
1981	The Role of Faith in the Process of Healing	SCM, London, Winston Press, Minneapolis, Harper and Row, San Francisco
1981	La Muerte Y el Morir	Fondo Educativo Internaciano—Madrid
1981	An Accidental Death	in What Helped Me When My Loved One Died, Earl Grollman, Ed., Beacon Press, Boston
1982	The Pastoral Counselor and the Child Encountering Death	In Helping Children Cope with Death, Hannelore Wass & Charles Carr, Ed., Hemishpere Publishing Co., Washington, NY
1982	Ages and Stages	Methodist Publishing House, Nashville
1982	Doubting is not Enough	with Marshall Dimock, SCM Press, London
1983	Första Sin Ensamhet	Verbumforlag, Sweden
1986	Your Health and You	Augsburg, Minneapolis
1989	Conquering Disability	Augsburg, Minneapolis
1989	Understanding Health	SCM Press, London, Trinity Press International, Philadelphia
2007	A Mystic Looks at Life	Trafford Publishing

Index:

.

Printed in the United States
by Baker & Taylor Publisher Services